How to Get the Most

BANG for your BUCK

IN THAILAND

CONTENTS

Chapter 1: INTRODUCTION

About Me

Privacy is a topic that is discussed at length in this book. I have mastered a system whereby I can stay in touch with my family and friends without anyone ever knowing about my little "hobby." Keeping this common goal in mind, you will find the amount of personal information about me to be limited. But here is what you need to know:

I am on the younger side of "middle-aged," and I am from the U.S. I had a small but reasonably successful business in the States for many years. I have never been married and I don't have children. I was with a woman in the U.S. for about a decade and the relationship was far from ideal, which should come as no surprise. Before settling down with my now ex-fiancé, I was reasonably successful with women, but certainly no Casanova. About five years ago, I bought a house with this woman and we were planning our wedding. She drove me crazy, but I was excited to start a family. A year later she was gone, my house was gone, my parents were gone, my youth was gone, and my business was in trouble... It was the perfect shit-storm.

Following that was a year during which I tried to put my life back together. Feeling lousier than I've ever felt, I remember sitting down one day and literally mapping out the steps to get back to some level of happiness. My plan was to solidify my business and even get a part-time job to get my finances together. I also planned to start going to the gym, and re-do my wardrobe a bit. I was going to start hanging out with the guys again, start dating, meet a girl who would treat me a lot better than my ex, and start a healthy relationship that could blossom into marriage. I was ready

and nothing was going to stop me, right? I really did try, I swear I did. But the reality was me being home alone almost every night. I found it nearly impossible to meet a girl while my personal bills and my business overheads were rising to a point of causing me terrible stress. It was impossible to find time for the gym because of the added hours of work I needed to put in to make ends meet. And hanging out with the guys? My friends were are all so bullied by their wives or so stressed out about their own finances that I was lucky if I got a night out with a friend every two months. And when my single friend and I did go out a few times, it was a lost cause. Being surrounded by young people and young women was just a twisted tease to us because we had no shot. They belonged to the happy young guys we used to be who hadn't been beaten down by Western Society yet.

So there I was: an overweight, financially troubled, stressed, physically and mentally unhealthy aging man. My best attempt at putting my life back together was a terrible failure and I was flat-out depressed. I was beginning to accept that my best years were behind me and I barely had enough energy to make new plans. My life consisted of working, taking care of my dog, watching TV, and feeling bad for myself. My bleak future was impacting me mentally. "Oh, that's what an anxiety attack is," I told myself.

One of my very best friends was divorced a handful of years before all of this. His entire life fell apart, and at a certain point he stopped answering phone calls from any of his friends. For a few months I played the part of a good friend and made every attempt to help the guy, but he wasn't interested in being helped and I hadn't talked to him in years. At my own rock-bottom, my friend called me. It had been a long time and I was very happy to hear from him, but something was different; he had so much energy, he was so upbeat and in such a great mood! I said, "What the hell happened to you?" He wouldn't even talk about it on the phone but demanded that we go out for drinks to catch up. Little did I know this encounter would have a more profound impact on me than any moment before it in my life.

So we met at a popular chain restaurant/bar and he immediately says, "Mike, you look like shit." I told him everything that had happened to me over the last two years and it felt good just to get it off my chest. It's not like I could afford the $200-per-hour shrink visits, so this was the first time I really let it all out.

I said, "Enough about me. You look like a million bucks. You must have met someone." He put down his beer and gave me the most sincere smile I have ever seen out of the man and said, "Mike, I went to Thailand for a month back in March and I just got back from spending another two weeks there."

And that was it. It really was as simple as that. Yes, we talked for hours that night about Thailand, but he had me at the first line. This man was glowing; he was BACK in every way and I was as happy for him as I was envious. So the minute he said "Thailand," I was sold. I was going to check this place out and see it for myself, no matter what. I was a desperate man so what could I lose?

He told me he was going out there again in six months and that we should go together, but I couldn't wait that long; I was falling apart and I needed some sort of help immediately. I left for Thailand a month after seeing my friend that night. Then, two weeks later I came back and I began to make piles of things I would sell, things I would store, and things I would take with me... **because I was moving to Thailand!**

Thailand immediately changed my life, and the best thing about it was that the metaphorical chains I was in were forever broken, and I was free to be the man I had always wanted to be and always should have been.

So just a couple of years later, as I write this, I am proud to say the following ten things about myself:

1) I have had more loving relationships with women in thirty months than any of my friends have had in their lives x 2, and that's being conservative. I literally fall in love all of the time.

2) I have been with more beautiful women in thirty months than all of my friends will ever be with in their lifetimes, combined.

3) I am in the best shape I have ever been in. I am considerably healthier than I could have ever dreamed about being. My hair even grew back! I have never looked or felt this good.

4) I have no debt and hardly any bills; I've forgotten what financial stress is like. I can live ten times better here than I did in the U.S., and for a tenth of the cost. In Thailand I am set for life financially, and it didn't take much for that to be the case.

5) My relationships with friends and family have never been better. I have re-connected with so many of my old friends, and when I visit the States there are never enough days to see all of the people that want to spend time with me. They're all so intrigued by my transformation and by my adventures!

6) Whenever I am back in the States I get laid frequently and easily. In fact there have been a number of women who want to visit me in Thailand and even move in with me there. Of course I always say no, but boy the tides have turned! Women can pick up that there is not a single desperate bone in my body and they are attracted to this.

7) I have taken up countless new hobbies such as wind surfing, water skiing, hiking, biking, kayaking, kickboxing, and golfing. These hobbies are all so cheap here and the scenery can be breathtaking.

8) I have the social life of a popular 18-year-old. I'm able to have nights out with the guys, take women out, or have people over for dinner as frequently as I can manage. Of course I still have the most incredible wild nights one can imagine whenever I get the urge, and that can be done any day of the week for about the

same price as buying a pay-per-view boxing event at home. Additionally, when a friend comes into town to visit me they have the time of their life, and I enjoy myself as I always do.

9) I have zero stress in my life now.

10) I am so thankful and so happy to be able to live this lifestyle, and I thank God nearly every day for this blessing.

What does my experience mean to you?

I found happiness in Thailand very quickly. Considering the position I was in before I came here, and knowing that there were currently tens of millions of men who were in a similar position, I began outlining this book early on, feeling compelled to help other people. So this collection of facts, tips, tricks, and experiences has taken years to put together, and it is far and away the greatest work of my life in every way.

I was happy from day-one in Thailand, but it took serious work to reach the pinnacle of my life where every aspect of my being is efficient, healthy, and happy. From point A (me crying on my couch in the U.S.) to point Z (me being on top of the world in every way in the most beautiful place in the world) was a process that took years of trial and error. For you, there will be no trial and there is no reason for error. The steps are laid out for you to follow and be as happy as you could have ever imagined, and that is whether you intend to come to Thailand on holidays, for extended holidays, or for good.

I have quasi-interviewed hundreds, and more likely thousands of people from all walks of life here in search of the best information that exists. I have asked the questions nobody else has. And I have asked them to every type of personality you'll find here, including rich tourists, rich ex-pats, poor ex-pats, budget tourists, bar girls, lady boys, hookers with more money than most foreigners, the most beautiful women in town, street walkers, drug addicts, bar owners, Russian escorts, shop owners etc. I have talked to and questioned every type, and I'll give myself credit for being good at getting honest answers from everyone across the board. I have also conducted hundreds of experiments with the notion of adding any pertinent information to this book that might be out there.

There is no stone left unturned and there is nothing I am leaving out. Regardless of your goals in Thailand, this book will help you in every way from the minute you start thinking about your next stint here (however long that may be) and beyond. It will certainly go too in-depth for many people on some topics, so feel free to skip around the book. I would rather have too much information than not enough.

My dilemma

"Mike, you can't honestly try and tell us that you're doing this just out of the goodness of your heart!"

There are a lot of factors that I've considered over time when it came to weighing up the advantages and disadvantages of writing this book.

Advantages:

1) I will pick up extra cash by selling copies each month.
2) I am changing people's lives in an extremely positive way.
3) I am fulfilling a lifelong dream of writing a book.
4) I have an excuse to do crazy things here in the interests of the book.

Disadvantages:

1) The costs of making and marketing the book, as well as for conducting my experiments for the book, are high and I may never break even.
2) The time I put into writing this is significant. I'll never be fairly compensated for this time.
3) The more people I give this information to, the more competitive I make things for myself here.
4) This is not a book I can ever show to my friends and family, and it will not be a part of my legacy. It may do a lot of people a lot of good, but it will mostly go uncredited.

So when I line those up, I guess it's pretty even. At times I think the disadvantages start to tip the scale, especially when I'm at home writing on a beautiful day when I could be out on the beach with a beautiful Thai girl.

I thought about the pros and cons, but ultimately there never was a decision making process, because I always felt compelled to do this from the moment I conceived the notion. It is simply something I had to do, and once I'd started it I certainly wasn't going to stop. As I write this I have already put in so many hundreds of hours outlining and making notes for each section of what is to follow, and in doing so I can honestly say that this whole process has made me reflect on every aspect of my life and life in general. This has helped to strengthen all of my abilities and my perception of things. So although it might be difficult to specify or quantify the personal benefits of creating this, they exist. There is no doubt that the process has been more enjoyable and fulfilling

than anything I have been a part of.

My Disclaimer

It is very important for me to leave no person feeling that they aren't part of the "proper demographic" for this book. That is why it is so in-depth and so detailed. But there is a big difference between a nice guy who wants to meet a sweet and innocent country woman in Thailand, and a party animal who wants to come here and do things that he'll never be able to talk about with his family and most of his friends. There is unbelievable information for you in the pages ahead, regardless of where you fall on the party-animal scale. Remember, no stone left unturned; I tackle every aspect of every topic. So I will mention yet again that you can feel free to skip around, and I understand that not every section will appeal to every reader.

Who is this book for?

This book can be of use to any man between the ages of 18 and 90. That may sound like a leap of faith on my part. It's understandable why a middle-aged or aging, single or divorced man with no children or older children would want access to this information, but why would a married man, or a young man, or a man with young children want to read this book? The simple answer is that every man deserves to know what life could be like in a better world.

I believe you can make Thailand your own personal paradise, and many people agree with me. This is no longer possible for most people in Europe or in North America. The economic climate has forever changed in these places, and so has society. Is it a secret that women in Asia treat men well or that women in the West don't? Is it a secret that no amount of money seems like enough anymore? The quality of life for the average man just isn't the same as it used to be, and it's only getting worse. People have to work harder and for more hours just to make the same money, and only to watch as food, gas and entertainment fees double and triple. Women have every advantage when it comes to relationships, and especially if there is a "divorce" involved. If you're not rich and you're not Brad Pitt, can you marry the most beautiful girl in town? Can you even talk to a pretty lady in a bar without feeling incredibly awkward and out of place?

You've read this far so it's safe to assume that you know Thailand has a lot to offer that your home town does not. Whether you are contemplating a dream vacation, an extended and annual or semi-annual trip, trial relocation, or permanent retirement, I have you covered. This book contains everything you could ever want to know about how it works here, why it works here, and thousands of tricks and tips to help you get everything you deserve out of every dollar, pound, or baht.

If you're young you owe it to yourself to spend some time here before you get crushed by Western Society. You will never be the same and you'll be much more successful with women and in life,

even just after a few weeks spent here. You'll see how far money can really go and you'll see just how WANTED you are by many women (especially Thai girls). Your perspective will change and you'll value money and you'll value yourself in a very healthy way.

If you're older and you have a little money, you can live the most luxurious lifestyle ever imagined, and you'll own the town.

If you're on a budget, there are hundreds of money saving tips in this book. Thailand can be so cheap as long as you avoid the tourist traps that are thoroughly discussed in this book. You can have the ultimate vacation here for a lot cheaper than you think. And if you are planning on spending a lot of time here or are already living here, this book should help you to increase your quality of life while cutting your budget in half. Even the most seasoned Thailand veterans will find useful tips and tricks scattered all throughout the book.

If you're unsure if Thailand is for you, as somewhere for a vacation or an extended stint, you will soon figure out your next step. I give you the good, the great, the bad, and the ugly; it's totally unfiltered. I'm not trying to sell you on Thailand (Thailand sells itself), I'm only giving you every piece of information you could ever need to know to get the most out of your experience here in every way.

If you're married but unhappy, find a way to come here. Tell her you're going to China for a week, and when you arrive in China pay for a flight to Bangkok in cash. Recharge your batteries here so you can go back to your old life refreshed, OR use your time here as a stepping stone to start a new life.

If you intend to spend one or two weeks here you have no time to waste experimenting. Read this cover to cover by the time you land, and you won't need to waste a single baht or hour experiencing anything other than the best this country has to offer.

If you're looking for love, I will tell you everything you need to know about what to look for and what to look out for. You can find your soul mate here, but if you're not careful you can become a victim. I explain how to put the ball in your court so you can get the right woman and begin a healthy relationship with her.

If you're gay or curious I have a section for you as well. It's fascinating how open this place is sexually, and if you're having a rough time with your sexuality in the States, I have the information you are looking for. There isn't a section of any book that covers any gay-friendly information like this. If you're not gay, you can just skip this section, but you may find it interesting.

If you're interested in opening a business here you will find this book to be an invaluable resource. I provide practical information and statistics for you as well as the do's and don'ts.

If you're depressed, unsatisfied, or unhappy, the plan you can make as a result of reading this book is the solution.

If you just want to do crazy things very cheaply with a lot of beautiful Thai women who all want you to marry them, then rest assured, you are reading the right book.

How to use this book

This is not a novel you have your hands on! There is no plot, no character development, and no surprise ending. It's simply the most extensive insider guide to Pattaya and Thailand in existence. You can certainly read it from front to back as most people do, but you can also feel free to skip around based on the topic headers that interest you most. Either way, it should become your handy reference guide, and you can use it as a tool indefinitely.

Locations covered

Most of the information in the book applies to all of Thailand, but in the interest of being thorough, I have added specific sections for separate places, which all include comparisons in terms of price, quality of women, etc. I discuss Pattaya, Bangkok, Chang Mai, and Phuket, in addition to a few other popular destinations. Living in Thailand for years, I have been to each of these places many times and I have interviewed lifers there. This is in addition to a tremendous amount of research that I have done across the board. I have you covered, whether you're coming to Phuket, Bangkok, Chiang Mai, Pattaya or you're just bouncing around. I also mention other places of interest in Thailand such as Koh Samuit, Koh Chang, Koh Tao, Koh Phangan, Koh Yai, and Krochanaburi, with the details you need to know about each.

"Why Pattaya?"

Thailand is an amazing place from top to bottom and there is something unique about each of its islands and cities. People never finish exploring Thailand for this reason. Living here I have made it a point to visit every place worth my time, but I always come back to my home base, Pattaya. Pattaya has a reputation for being a bit sleazy and for the beach not being clean. Good! This reputation is what keeps it from being too highly populated with foreigners (farang). Don't get me wrong, there are still a lot of farang here, but the #'s are overwhelmingly in our favor, meaning there are still way more of them (Thai girls) than there are of us!

There is simply no other place in the world that is like Pattaya. Here you will have the opportunities that people don't think exist, and at prices that people shake their head at. There is a very nice beach five minutes away (10 baht by "baht bus") called Jomtien, and there is a spectacular beach island called Koh Larn which is a quick 30-baht boat ride away from the pier. Did I mention that Pattaya has more available women than any other location in the world? Or that if you walk for a few minutes you will see what it's like to be George Clooney? Some people say it's Disney Land for men, but when I was a child, Disney was never even close to this much fun.

More than that, Pattaya has something for everyone. Great food, great shopping, Western restaurants, suburban sections, modern malls and movie theatres, water sports, and everything else you could ever want are all easily found. You get a little bit of everything, and its one of the cheapest tourist-friendly places in the world. The nightlife can be as wild as any, but you can go to nice restaurants away from the craziness anytime you'd like.

I think Pattaya makes for the premier "guy-only vacation spot" in the world, and I also think it's a superior place to live. It's close enough to Bangkok (120 baht by bus, 1,000 baht by taxi); Jomtien and Koh Larn give it some beach character; and it's not terribly far from Koh Chang which is a fantastic island.

There is a good chance if you're reading this that I don't even need to convince you to make Pattaya a priority on your list of places to go. You are probably well aware of this gem, and if you're not then make sure you check it out for yourself.

Pattaya girls can also be a handful compared to other Thai women, so it's important you know some basics before getting involved with them. Whether you just have a couple of days here or you live here, I have all of the information you could ever need about Pattaya and Pattaya girls. I delve into areas that have never been discussed at length in print before.

Questions

I also wanted to have a special feature for my readers that would take interaction to a whole new level. I know I didn't miss a beat in this book, but there are so many different types of people out there and it's possible that you have a question or two that the book does not cover. For this reason, any of my customers can email in a question or two and I will sincerely try to give you the best possible answer or solution.

When you bought this book you received a confirmation code. Email info@thaigirlspattayagirls.com and be sure to put the confirmation code from your purchase in the subject. In the body, include your questions. All of my customers get one good crack at a Thailand and Pattaya expert. Thailand girls, Pattaya girls, business… You can ask me anything!

Competitors/Other books

I realize that there are other books out there and it is very important to me to bring a lot to the table that none of these do. Many of the books you'll find were written five years before this one. Pattaya and Thailand has changed so much in the last few years that these older books are obsolete. But most importantly I noticed that none of my competitors have been as thorough as potential readers would want, so I have covered that shortfall for you. I give you ten times more tricks, more examples, and more information. As such, this resource is more valuable to you than all of the competition combined.

Chapter 2: THAI GIRLS

The women in Thailand are unrecognizable from the women back home, and I'm not just talking physically. There are always exceptions, but the majority of Thai women are peaceful Buddhists who are eager to take good care of a man. Living in an island-like environment helps to give them exotic looking features and slim waistlines. They are known for having a healthy sexual appetite and for being somewhat submissive. If you ask a Thai girl what she would like to do on any given night, she is likely to reply, "Up to you." A large percentage of the women grow up without much privilege or luxury, if any. So if they are pretty they will have an opportunity to cash in on those looks from the time they are of age (and unfortunately sometimes sooner).

When Westerners visit Thailand they almost exclusively interact with bar girls or Gogo dancers. It sets up nicely this way because these women are very good at showing a foreign man a good time and making them feel appreciated. Bar girls and Gogo dancers are usually willing to exit their line of work if they meet the right man, and they usually aren't overly picky about that process. But we must never forget one thing: bar girls and Gogo dancers are prostitutes. They are the minority in Thailand as most women in the country have never been paid for sex. Bangkok, Pattaya, and Phuket are inundated with "pay-for-play" women because these are obviously the most lucrative places for them to work. Don't let anyone tell you differently. If someone says, "Every girl in Thailand has her price," they simply don't know the facts. Estimates on the amount of prostitutes in Thailand vary widely, from between 150,000 to 2 million. I suspect the smaller number is a bit of wishful thinking for those that intend to give the country the benefit of the doubt. Most likely it is somewhere in between, but even if it was 2 million, that would still be around 3% of the population which certainly does not equate to 6% of women, as male prostitutes account for their fair share of the total. It might be safe to assume that from 3 to 5 per cent of women here have been in the industry at some point. You wouldn't know it if you went to the most traveled tourist locations, but it's true. So, combining themes, we see that 90 per cent of the men that visit are only interacting with 3 to 5 per cent of the female population.

There was a poll here among foreign men that asked if they had any reservations about marrying a woman who was at some point in the "bar girl" industry in Thailand, and the majority of men actually said it would not be a problem to them. I suspect this is for two reasons: 1) non-prostitutes from their own countries probably treat them worse and try to get more money out of them than prostitutes do in Thailand; and 2) they believe Thai prostitutes are forced into the industry out of poverty and therefore should be forgiven. Is this accurate? Only on the surface. They will treat you well and for fairly little money in the beginning, but that all changes if the long-term switch is flicked. And although it's true that some Thai women have no choice but to work in the industry because they have to support a dozen starving people from their village, the reality is that 90 per cent of the bar girls could have done something else but instead chose the easier option.

I always suggest that you have fun and enjoy your time with bar girls to your heart's content. But if you're looking for a long-term relationship or marriage, you should stay away from the touristy spots and from the bars. I will of course break this down for you in the coming chapters, but try to keep this in mind as a rule of thumb.

Bar Girls

You're not likely to get very far in Thailand without seeing some "girl bars" or GoGo's. Each establishment is designed for foreign men to come in, buy some drinks, pick out a lady, buy the lady some watered down drinks, and then pay the bar to leave with the lady, and lastly pay the lady for her time, either short or long. Of course, short-time is for up to two hours, and long-time is until the morning if you want it to go that long. For non-high-end establishments (discussed next), a typical bar fine is 300 to 500 baht, and the girls charge from 700 to 1,000 for short-time, and 1,000 to 1,500 for long-time. They get paid when you buy them a drink and they usually keep the money you give them. Some ask for a tip, but only if they know you're a rookie. They usually have minimums for drinks they have to sell in one night, if not a quota set by the bar then at least as a personal goal. The money they get paid for "lady drinks" is probably enough for them to live on, and the money they get from their customers is usually split on some combination of family, clothing, food, and waste.

Easily more than 50 per cent of these girls have at least one child that their Mother looks after in their home town. You can usually see who has a child and who doesn't if you get a good shot at their body. Since they are petite, there is often some damage leftover as a result of childbirth, either to their abdomen or their breasts. Usually the child has a Thai father who is completely out of the picture, and a small percentage of them have a child with a farang who is also out of the picture. It should be noted that a portion of these women are still with their boyfriends or husbands. These men look past and accept what their wife does for a living, or in some instances they push their wife to do it because of the sheer earning potential.

The dynamic of family and how it relates to the Thai "working girl" is sometimes hard to swallow. In a best-case scenario the family accepts money each month from their daughter because they need it, and they just ignore and avoid the topic of how the money is made. In the worst case, they are pushed into it by their parents who see it as the easiest way to improve the quality of their own lives without having to do anything. It's a different world here, and therefore prostitution is looked at differently, especially as a means to an end concerning poverty.

A large percentage of the bar girls are from a North Eastern region of Thailand, called Isan. This is a very poor area of Thailand, and for whatever reason it is rich in one resource, pretty girls. Many of the girls work in hard-labor jobs in a factory or on a farm and are not properly educated. They can come to a tourist hot-spot and start making five to ten times as much money as they did in their old lives. Some of them work the busy season as a bar girl and then go back to their home town and work again, while spending time with their family. It was explained to me that the largest crop harvests coincide with the least busy holiday times (by coincidence), so many of them are not needed around their family's farm during the busiest tourist seasons.

After a bar girl has been in the industry for a while, she may be street-tough and never as innocent and appealing as before, but the majority of them still have a good heart and no bad intentions. I think this is a reason why Thai prostitutes have such a better reputation in their society than Western prostitutes do. Here they blend into society, and Thai people generally don't judge them, while in our home countries they don't want anyone to ever find out what they do or else they will be forever shunned. Surely the bar girls here mean well for the most part. It's a large group of lazy and semi-attractive women who don't look at men as they should, but aren't at all "bad people." With that said, there are certainly exceptions, and there are horror stories where innocent farang fall victim to bar girls and their associates. If you finish reading this book, you have no chance to be the victim, but we must address what to look out for, and I do so in continuing chapters.

Many bar girls and some dancers also try and line up what they call "sponsors" for themselves. Really the more appropriate term would be "sucker." Many farang fall in love with a pay-for-play girl, and the girls are good at convincing them that the feeling is mutual. Then when it's time for the man to go back home to his job (or maybe even his family), the girl will put on a show, explaining how she doesn't want to work in the bar anymore or have to see other men because she is so in love. The man might ask how much money it would cost per month for the woman to stop working in the industry, and she may say anything from 15,000 to 30,000 baht per month, then maybe they negotiate down to anywhere from 10,000 to 20,000 baht per month. Now in theory this doesn't sound all that bad, and that is why so many of these women actually do have a sponsor or sponsors. Three-hundred to six-hundred U.S. dollars per month to support a woman who you are in love with to keep her loyal to you and out of a terrible line of work sounds like a bargain. She'll talk to you on web cam and send you emails and pictures, and she'll be here waiting for you whenever you make it back out to Thailand. The problem is that she'll also still be working at the bar and she'll still be going home with customers each night. You may not even be her only "sponsor." If she tells you she's not seeing any men, she's lying. Some of these women have three sponsors who all send money to the woman thinking they're the only man in their lives, while the women continue to get bar-fined with new men and new potential "sponsors." I have seen bar girls laugh at their sponsors behind their back; it's revolting. They justify it by telling themselves that the man is just lying to them and he also has other ladies, maybe even a wife at home, and certainly other Thai girls. In some situations, this is certainly true and the farang and bar girls just lie to each other. But there are some men who don't have any ladies at home, and who have given up all other Thai ladies. These men really have fallen in love with the girl and are willing to be good to her. These men get it bad. There's just about no scenario where paying a bar girl a monthly stipend will ever work out well. You are not only wasting money, you're being taken advantage of. I can expand on what happens in the long run, as many of these situations progress, but it's pointless. Nothing good ever happens and you should never become a sponsor. If you are a sponsor as you read this, cut the woman off permanently.

I have met lovely girls at bars in Thailand, you can be sure of that. I wouldn't marry one and I don't think you should, especially if they have been in the industry for more than a couple of months. If you compare bar girls as "marriage material" to typical women from back home, I suppose it would be close and the bar girls may even come out on top. However, a Thai girl who never worked the bars is easily the far superior option in terms of a long-term companionship.

But one thing is for sure, a night with a good bar girl in Thailand is about ten times more fun and satisfying than one with a hooker from back home. You have no buyer's remorse, because you spent a tenth of the money, and because you and the girl genuinely had a good time. Make no mistake about it, the element of the bar scene is one of the best and most unique things about

Thailand. If you know what to look for and you don't fall into one of the traps (like sending them Western Unions for their sick uncle), then their existence enables us to have as much fun or short-term companionship as we could ever need. Those that know the system just hope for one thing: that it never changes.

Rookie

You can figure out how long a girl has been in the industry by the amount of English that she speaks. If she's fluent in English and even in slang, then she has been doing it for years. If she barely speaks a word of English, she's most likely been in the industry for a short time. Simply asking the girl how long she's worked in the scene is not even close to an exact science. Most girls will lie about this because they believe the longer they've worked in the bar, the more of a whore you think they are. You are better off going on instincts and clues. How comfortable is she around the bar, with you or with her bar girl friends? Does she know any slang? Does she seem to have a Western sense of humor? Is she shy at all? Does she have multiple tattoos? Girls straight out of Isan have no understanding of Western humor such as sarcasm, they're incredibly shy, they don't know any English, and they won't understand a lick of slang.

There are two benchmarks for the cycle of a girl's entrance into the bar-girl scene. The first is once she has had her first good experience with a man whose encounter lasted forty-eight hours or more, or perhaps for the duration of the man's holiday. At this point it's likely that she was treated better than she has ever been treated before by a man who she honestly likes, and she was paid handsomely for her time. This changes a girl. Now she knows she can get paid nicely just for enjoying herself and she has the opportunity to meet great guys in the process. She'll never be the same again. It should be noted that if you are that man, the man a bar girl has her first strong connection with, you are getting an untainted girl, and I believe the couple of weeks she was in the business prior can be overlooked, as can her decision to enter the business in the first place. I base this on other people's experiences. It is not uncommon for a girl to enter the scene and quit shortly after when she meets her first special farang, and the success rate of these relationships is fairly high. Of course this would happen more if it wasn't for the fact that most of these men are on vacation and go home shortly after. They may or may not try to keep a long-distance relationship going, but this never works, and the girl is right back into the scene a changed woman.

The second bench mark for a bar girl is usually at about the three- to four-month marker. By now she has had many customers, short-time and long-time, and she has also been with multiple men who she liked and probably thought she loved. She is no longer a rookie and she has been hardened by the system. She knows that she can get what she wants from men if she's slick about it, so now she is always putting on a show, at least to some degree. She has also seen men she likes come and go, thus she is also jaded by the illusions of the "girlfriend experience" and by love. Her feelings on trust and loyalty are supplanted by skepticism and greed. By this point she has abandoned many of her Thai traditions, and there isn't much left of the innocent girl who was on a bus a few months earlier wondering what Buddha had in store for her. Fortunately, Thai culture and tradition is too rich to be completely abandoned, and most of the bar girls still have some sort of special connection to their roots.

Gogo Dancers

The difference between the average Gogo dancer and the average bar girl is this: A Gogo dancer makes more money (sometimes much more), has less freedom and flexibility in her schedule, and has to work harder. This is why every now and then you find a beautiful girl in a bar despite the money being inferior; some of them prefer sitting down and almost being able to choose who they go home with at the bar, as opposed to dancing in heels all night and waiting until a man purchases them. While it's true that some bar girls really are looking to meet a husband, that can't be said of a Gogo dancer. They can't date and go to dinner without you having to buy them out, they have no day off for you and they're always on the clock. I'm not saying it's impossible; I have personally bought out Gogo dancers for long periods of time and could have taken care of them from there on out if I had wanted to. But surely, meeting a husband cannot be their priority if they're in a Gogo. Money is absolutely their priority. They may not even charge or cost much more than a bar girl on the first night; perhaps a little more on the bar fine and a little more on the short-time/long-time. It's their sheer volume (sometimes two or more customers in a night) that takes them up a level in pay. In any bar during the week, a pretty girl may go home alone (especially after the busy season), but that won't happen in a Gogo.

Some dancers are topless, completely nude, or wear bikinis or sexy costumes. The laws are confusing, and every now and then you'll see a bar get shut down and fined for a night due to nudity, so I guess it's tolerated but not necessarily legal. Actually, being technical, the same can be said for prostitution in Thailand in general.

There is also a known drug problem in the Gogos; more so than in the bars. The girls don't dance in shifts like at the strip clubs back home; they're all on the stage at all times because they're seen as merchandise to the owners. I suppose there is where the excuse to partake in drugs comes from (not that strippers from back home don't have a reputation for being into drugs). But it is hard to dance for an audience for so many hours every day of your life without the occasional pick-me-up. I can't say what percentage of girls actually do drugs. I have tried to figure that out and its one of the most perplexing things I have come across. I have had people "in the know" tell me its 10 per cent and others tell me its 50 per cent or more. We do know one thing for sure, it is almost impossible to tell who is and who isn't using drugs unless they're a complete degenerate. Girls from back home go through obvious physical changes with their weight when they are on drugs, and their faces usually look terrible. Because the girls here are already so slim, and because many of them put on a lot more makeup than would be acceptable back home, you really can't tell.

Most dancers have the same routine. They all live in a small apartment with at least one other girl and most of them share a bed with another girl. They can afford to have their own bed but sharing a bed with family and friends is very common here. They wake up around 3pm, and they spend what's left of their day eating, watching TV, shopping, and getting ready to go work, which takes a long time. As I mentioned before, they think it's ok to use large amounts of makeup, and since they use cheap stuff, this begins to have a negative impact on their face. Naturally, they don't make it any better by putting more and more on to cover blemishes that come as a result, and so it becomes a bad cycle. The gravedigger shift isn't healthy to begin with, and then all that sweat with the cheap makeup causes the real damage. This is why when you wake up the next morning with a dancer, you may be surprised by what you see. If they like you, sometimes they'll make sure to exchange phone numbers with you and escape your room before you see them without their mask. I make a point of this because it's a well-known problem. This isn't a national problem. Thai girls don't have bad skin; Gogo dancers have bad skin.

One thing any veteran to the Gogo scene knows is that these girls can all eat. I guess their bodies require large portions of carbohydrates thanks to the physical nature of their job, but I have never seen girls eat so much food and stay in such amazing shape. If you take the bar-fine plunge and spend a few days with a Gogo girl you will get a kick out of watching them eat.

High-end Gogo Dancer

If a girl has an amazing body, a beautiful face, or she is a very talented dancer, she will probably work her way up to the higher-end Gogos. These aren't the Gogos that offer 50-baht beer specials. These places charge nearly double for drinks and bar fines. The bar fines go up to 1,000, and the short-time/long-time split can be as high as 2,000 to 3,000. Do the math and 4,000 baht will get you the sexiest pay-for-play specialist in the business.

There is a very small exception worth mentioning: there are stunning girls (10s) who consider themselves, "high-class working girls" usually out of Bangkok, who operate almost like escorts do back home. Some of them will pop up in a Gogo once in a while and they don't want to be bar-fined, but they'll let you take them out to dinner where a real shakedown will ensue at typical Western prices. There are also Eastern European women who work in the same way, but I mention them in another chapter. I'm not saying you can find a good long-term thing with a girl at the high-end Gogo establishments, because it's very difficult and probably not worth it; but I am saying that it's completely impossible to make it work with the "high-class working girls" who know they're a 10. A lot of wealthy Japanese men pay big money for these women to be their vacation mates. I took a flight from Tokyo to Bangkok one time and I noticed about ten beautiful Thai women traveling alone on that flight. I suppose some of them become semi-mistresses to rich men in Japan. You may get the opportunity to have a fun day or week with a girl like this, but you can get a high-priced whore anywhere in the world just the same, so I don't see the point. You also may never come into contact with a girl like this, because it has only happened to me a few times.

Back to the high-end Gogo girls. I believe there is a place for them in your vacation routine or in your monthly budget if you live here. They're the sexiest girls you're going to find who will go home with you and no questions asked. You can have the time of your life with them for a night, or maybe even a couple of nights, but past that, you're not getting anything accomplished with a girl like this.

If the best looking and fastest talking man in the world came to one of these high-end establishments and tried to do everything he could to make a girl like him, that girl would still probably charge him the same daily and weekly rates as any man who was 100 pounds or 50 kilos overweight, and who couldn't even come close to getting laid at home. I'm not saying that you can't make it work with a beautiful Gogo dancer, but be prepared to spend, and be prepared to not get treated as well as you would by most other Thai women. I personally question the motivation for trying, as you can get a beautiful woman who is loyal and honest and has never sold themselves if you're willing to put just a little bit of work into it and you go to a non-tourist spot. Again, I enjoy a night with a beautiful Gogo dancer as much as anyone, but I know my limit. After a certain point it's no longer fun to be looked at like an ATM machine, and if I wanted that I should have stayed in the U.S. For me, that mark is right around fifteen hours. So I have them for the entire night and through lunch the next day, and then when she asks me if I want to bar-fine her for another night, I might say yes at my weakest moment with the most beautiful of Gogo girls, but usually I am able to just say no. An exception would be a special-occasion weekend trip to an island or something like that, but in those instances I set ground rules and prices ahead of time, and I never pay more than 50 per cent until the very end of the time that we agreed on.

You can enjoy yourself to no end with a beautiful dancer, and you can meet one and go home with one and feel loved by one at the drop of a hat; there are hundreds available for you at any given time. This is enticing and amazing at times, but it is a dangerous temptation. This is why I urge you to never lose the proper perspective, which is that these girls are 75 per cent or more about the money. Thai girls can be among the most appreciative women in the world, but by chasing after beautiful Gogo dancers you are absolutely never going to be appreciated. They'll get what they can from you, and when you stop giving, they'll stop talking to you no matter how much you think they liked you, or even if they really did like you.

Some veterans may say that this is true of every pay-for-play lady in Thailand: that to be with them you'd better support their entire family and give them as good a lifestyle as any of their friends have been given by a farang. This is not totally true in the bars. There are at least some bar ladies who have money and love neck-and-neck in their priority list. But in the high-end Gogos, the "for love or for money" question is not in play; all of the ladies will always be in it with a farang for the money.

Street Walker

If you're a man with a budget, or a girl just happens to find you at the right place and the right time, you may have yourself an encounter with a street walker. These girls don't work in bars or in Gogos, but recruit clients on the street. So why would a girl work on the street and not in a bar or a Gogo? I will go from the best to worst reasons:

1) She wants to experiment and see what it's like without going through an entire job-application process.
2) She's a student or she has some type of legitimate job and likes to moonlight as a prostitute.
3) She has not and will not do this for a career but something has come up that has put her in a financial bind and she's willing to do this for some quick cash.
4) She enjoys flexibility. She does not want to do this on a set schedule and have to be some place seven days a week. She isn't interested in maximizing her revenue potential but just wants to work enough to make a living without having to punch a time-clock.
5) Her marriage or her children leave her only a short time to make extra cash.
6) She is not a woman, she just looks like one. I'll expand on this in an upcoming chapter.
7) She is not pretty enough to work at the bars and Gogos.

8) She has a bad drug problem; so bad that she can't stabilize any type of employment.
9) She has HIV and she can't pass the HIV test most establishments give to their employees.

Most of the street walkers fall into category 6 or category 7. I'm sure there are a decent amount of drug addicts in the mix too, and probably around 3 per cent have HIV, which is actually quite high.

So, knowing this, why might you be interested in a street walker?

1) They will go with you for a short time for 500 baht with no questions asked and you don't need to buy a "lady drink" or anything. It's the cheapest way to get off and it doesn't take a whole lot of time to find one.
2) If you really look and sort through all of the inferior streetwalkers, there is almost always a decent-looking one who fits somewhere into categories 1 to 4. Granted these girls don't last on the streets for long, and pick up customers usually within thirty minutes of standing in a spot, but they do exist. It's not easy to find them, but decent looking girls are available for 500 baht if you take the time to look.
3) They're willing to do things other girls may not be. I don't condone anything too crazy... I may not put it past some of these girls to do some the craziest of things imaginable for the right price, but don't go there. If we're talking about watching porn together, threesomes, or anal, that stuff may be in the mix with a street walker, but you need to make sure she is totally ok with it, and you always need to use protection. Do not under any circumstance try to get her to do something she does not want to wilfully do.
4) You want to experiment with a lady boy and are too embarrassed to go to an establishment. Not my cup of tea, but to each their own.

I prefer bars to the streets every time, but I can't completely write them off. This wouldn't be fair, because some people really are on a budget and there are a couple of winners on the street once in a while. I have been there and done that; a couple of times for experimentation and a couple of times because it was too late and all the bars were closed. I used protection and it was cheap, so I certainly never regretted the money spent. Of course some of the girls had body issues that I couldn't pick up on at first, and I always watched my wallet with them. I never went "long time" with one and I don't suggest you do. The best street walkers I ever went home with were on the nights when they were like finding a needle in a haystack. They were the girls who were not real pros, and I could tell were new. They're few and far between.

Perhaps the most important thing to know about streetwalkers is that they are more likely to do something malicious to you. This is obvious. If they work in a bar or Gogo, it doesn't take much to track them down and go to their boss. On the street it's a whole different story. Wallets have been known to disappear when guys fall asleep next to a street walker, and that shouldn't come as a surprise. Sometimes, in rare instances, you can have a problem worse than a missing wallet.

Freelancer/Club girl

It's hard to put an exact label on the girls you find at a dance club/disco. Certainly they are prostitutes, but past that you get kind of a mixed bag, and that can also depend on the disco itself.

Many bars close at 2 or 3am, and if the girls didn't find a customer, or they've finished with a short-time customer, they may still have ambition to make more money and decide to hit one of the afterhours discos. In some situations they may go to have some fun with their bar-girl friends while they look for customers, and they may care a little or a lot about finding a customer, depending on their mood and their desire for cash.

There are also some girls who get paid by the clubs, minimally, to freelance there, or at a minimum get paid for the drinks they sell. And you'll see many girls that don't have an arrangement with anybody but are pretty enough to be welcome into a disco to freelance. There are no bar fines in the discos; the clubs rely on the girls being there so they can sell drinks. These girls are usually somewhat attractive and can dance reasonably well. They're also somewhat choosey about who they go home with. I have had success with these women both short- and long-term. That's right; I did not say "time", I said "term". If you insist on being with a girl for a few weeks who comes from the "scene", this may be your best choice. If the girls go off for a week or more, it usually isn't a problem. There is no "buy out" or long-term bar fine. If the girl likes you she may not charge you to keep your company past the first night, and she'll just see to it that you send her parents whatever money she would have sent them in the time you're with her, in addition to covering her expenses, which may include food and rent for her apartment. After a week or so she may try to move in with you, and it may seem like a good idea to save some money. Don't do it. These relationships usually fizzle out after about a month. There will be some types of problem at that mark. Her phone will keep ringing with past customers, and you'll wonder what she's doing every moment that you're not together. She'll never get a real job, and if she goes back to the club just to "dance" or to "sell drinks", then it'll be over immediately.

Freelancers at a disco are different from street walkers, although they may occasionally cross paths. None of the discos have a problem kicking girls out if they're not the "club's type", which is a good thing. There are some decent-looking girls at the discos, same as in the bars. You won't see stunners unless they're there with a guy, but lots of 7s. They try and get what they can in terms of prices, so the charges do vary, but if you make it clear that you're not clueless, it should be around 800 for short-time and 1200 for long-time, to possibly 25 per cent higher than that if the girl is very cute. If they're having a good time and they like you, it's possible to get them down to 500 baht for short-time, and they may stay over just for your AC if they feel comfortable with you. In a way it can be the closest thing to the "girlfriend experience", because it's not completely fake, and a lot of the girls at the discos are looking for a man they can be with long-term.

The disco freelancer who is easily a level above any streetwalker, but who doesn't want the hassles of working a bar twenty-seven days a month, is a nice target for men on vacation. Cheap rates, no bar fines, and good companionship from a nice pretty lady make it a no brainer. These girls are ideal to take with you for a weekend as well. In many ways they're the best of the breed, but standard cautions still apply. They are prostitutes and they have probably sold themselves to hundreds of men. They have also been known to cause a problem or two since they don't have a boss to answer to each day. The bars and Gogos test their girls (at least they're supposed to) and these girls don't have to get tested. You can always get her tested at any clinic, but make sure you are smart about the whole process.

Non-prostitutes 1

Non-prostitutes who are very familiar with the "foreigner scene" and exclusively date foreigners.

There are women out there who want to meet a foreign man for some good and bad reasons, but are unwilling to partake in the "pay-for-play" bar/disco/Gogo scene. Girls who fit this bill still live in the same tourist hot-spots such as Koh Samuit, Phuket, Bangkok, and Pattaya. Many of them work in jobs where they interact with farang, possibly at a shopping mall, a restaurant, or a hotel. Some girls own their own shops or have good jobs and are financially solvent, but still seek a Western man because they believe they treat women well.

You could break this category of women into two groups: those who used to be prostitutes and those who never were. I'll tackle the women who used to be paid for sex, first. These girls who were in the industry might have saved enough money to be able to open their own shop and were happy to quit the pay-for-play scene. Others might have been tired of the scene, and some even more savvy women may have realized their best chance at landing a good man would be if they weren't prostitutes but had access to the men of the cities that are filled with prostitutes. The girls who used to be in the industry and somehow removed themselves from it, and are employed or have their own shop, are a notch above a prostitute in terms of long-term companionship, in my opinion, but they're never many notches above. You may have heard the phrase, "Once a whore, always a whore." That's a very negative saying, but there is some truth in it. If a woman is able to pry herself away from the scene successfully, she obviously cares about herself and her future, and she is most likely a battle-tested, strong, and independent woman. This is true, but she still sold herself to many men and that irrevocably changes a woman for the worse. There is no way she can ever look at men in the same away after being in that industry for more than a few months. Her love/money priority lines will always be disproportionate, and you are better off settling down with a girl who was never in the industry to begin with. I have nothing against dating a woman who fits this bill and seeing how it goes. But use limits.

Now, focusing on the other part of this group we have girls who have never been prostitutes and only want to be with farang. The first obstacle here is figuring out which group the girl belongs to, because if she used to work in a bar, don't expect her to tell you, even if you ask her—even if you ask her and say that it's ok if she did—even if you ask her and you say it's ok if she did and that if she lies you will never talk to her again—even if you tell her you have evidence that she worked in a bar and have video footage, Thai girls will always lie about their past as a prostitute. They know the minute they tell you they worked in a bar you will never look at them the same again, and it's probably true. That's a major problem with this group. You don't know what to believe and you will always question their intentions. For a woman to write off everyone except farang, so much so that she lives in a city primarily to find one, qualifies as suspect behavior in my book. (Yes, figuratively and literally... wah wah).

This is a tough group to call because of intentions, questions, lies, etc. You'll always think the lady wanted a farang to be financially secure, and you'll always feel that you were the guy stupid enough to give her that security. And you may be wrong. If a girl was treated terribly by her Thai father and her Thai brother, and slapped around by her first Thai boyfriend, and then made a pact with herself to only be with Western men who she sees as being totally loving and charming in the movies, could you blame her? And if that same girl never sells herself in a city where she easily could, but just positions herself to meet a good guy, could you blame her? What's wrong with that? Nothing is wrong with that, but it's almost impossible to tell if a girl really fits the criteria, and it's a bit of a long shot. Sure she may have some ex-boyfriends from the West who always try to get back in touch with her, and that will irritate you, but as long as she doesn't cheat on you this shouldn't be a problem, should it? Jealousy is toxic to any relationship, and it takes on an entirely different dynamic when it becomes international. When you had a girlfriend or wife back home, you knew she'd had ex-boyfriends and it didn't bother you. It doesn't bother you that your Thai girl had Thai ex-boyfriends either. But if your Thai girl has ex-boyfriends from the West it drives you nuts, especially if they think they're still in the picture. And many Western men always think they're in the picture with any Thai women they were with, and this can be noted as **"Annoying Farang Fact #1."** Many farang just don't understand when a woman is done with them, and despite it being obvious they continue to call and email their Thai ex-partner, and perhaps offer them money when they are truly desperate. Whether they are overly confident in thinking the girl will always be interested in them, or just desperate and heart-broken, either way it's bad, and either way it's annoying when you are dating a girl who is almost being harassed by some douche bag.

It's hard to find closure on what to think about a girl who isn't a prostitute but only dates farang, it really is. I don't even know if I know where I stand with it totally, but at least I have discussed every angle so that you can make your own decision. My gut tells me that if a girl is definitely not a prostitute, she insists she never was, and she doesn't have any prostitute friends, you might as well roll the dice. Her friends will tell the whole story. If she was in the industry, she made and keeps friends with the girls she met during that time.

One last important point about these girls is that many of them find foreign men on international dating web sites. Normally these sites don't charge the ladies to be on the site, but charge the men monthly. They're popular and have many thousands of members. There are some really bad stories of women just abusing men who they meet on these sites by talking to them for a couple of months and then asking for large amounts of money for emergencies. You probably don't need me to tell you that those are just scams, but, there are many nice Thai girls on these sites who fit the category of this section. They are not a bar girl, and they may or may not have ever been a bar girl. They know at least a little English and they want to find a foreign man. Some may have decent intentions and some may just be hunting for sponsors/suckers. I don't think this is a good way to meet a wife, and I don't think there is any point in just lining up some play dates for when you get to Thailand; doing that once you're here doesn't take a whole lot of effort. I think it provides men with a flavor of Thailand when they're in between vacations, and I can't blame them for wanting that. As I mentioned, there are also some good women on these sites, so I won't recommend or knock them.

I'm not even sure where I would classify a girl who works in a legitimate, non-happy-ending massage establishment. They're clearly looking for Western men. And the ones who work in a "happy-ending" massage spot are obviously in the same boat as other prostitutes in Thailand. I'll talk more about these places in the next chapter.

Non-prostitutes 2

Non-prostitutes who are traditional and have rejected opportunities to live in the fast lane.

I saved the best for last, and fortunately there are about 27 million women in Thailand who match these criteria. A real Thai woman who was never a prostitute and who never deliberately put herself in a position to meet only Farang—there is your ideal long-term mate. They can be a little rough around the edges in ways the bar girls aren't, but it's no big deal, and I'll explain.

Most country women are as peaceful as can be. They are ideally suited for taking care of a family, and this is what they strive to do. They have most likely worked hard in their lives, possibly even doing physical labor. By avoiding the bar world, they either work hard on a farm or in a factory, or better yet go to college so they can eventually get a proper desk job.

These are not money-hungry, selfish women we are talking about. They are sometimes selfless to a fault. They meditate and are intrigued by nature. Their family and their future family is their life. They take pleasure in taking care of people. Financial security is meaningful to Asian women as a whole, and they will look for this security in picking a future spouse, but this is natural and healthy as they want to make sure they are solidifying their future family's life. The bar girls will eventually look for more than just security, and there is an element of them getting whatever they can get, while the non-bar girls just seek basic security.

If they're not virgins when they get married, they're pretty close to it. There used to be a high percentage of the country women who were virgins until marriage, but that has been changing lately. Many good women are experimenting a bit more in their high-school years with their Thai schoolmates, but it is done so that their parents don't find out, and certainly not to excess. This ties into the dowry.

A dowry is a fee a family charges you if you marry their daughter. If she is a virgin, the dowry is higher, therefore some parents tell their children that they are not to ever have sex, and of course some of them do behind their parents' backs.

Most of these country women do not speak much English, and many of them do not know about modern-day Western rituals, such as shaving their legs or wearing the latest fashions. They are extremely shy and it can take weeks or even months for them to warm up to a man who doesn't speak Thai. It can be a heavy undertaking to meet a proper woman here in Thailand, and it's not recommended to attempt this in a short vacation unless you're specifically "wife-hunting."

You won't have a wild time with a country woman; many of them have never been in a bar and don't like alcohol. The women don't smoke and they don't have tattoos. They won't show you any public displays of affection even once they have warmed up to you. But, they are peaceful, loving, and caring women. They are not the type of women who will cause you any type of stress—a characteristic that should never be overlooked!

There is a lot for us to learn from traditional Thai women. Their spiritual ways and their connection with nature is just beautiful. Regardless of your personal religious beliefs, we can all learn something from Buddhism if it's practiced properly. I have known many women who say they "don't mind cooking," but true Thai women live to cook for you. Expect a healthy diet of exotic and tasty food if a country woman is regularly cooking for you.

I think these women make some of the most ideal wives and mothers you're likely to find around the globe. I also think that it will be a work in progress initially communicating with one, or even finding one in general, since they won't be frequenting the same spots you would be on a typical holiday. There is a chapter later in the book which goes through the steps necessary to find a woman like this for long-term companionship or marriage. If you're just looking to have a good time in Thailand, stick with the bar girls; they may not be marriage material, but they're a hell of a lot of fun. If you're looking for love, then you can read more about what to do in chapter 6.

Chapter 3: SHORT-TIME/LONG-TIME

This is an overview of the types of establishments with Thai girls you will find in Pattaya and all over

Thailand, and tips on how to go about picking these establishments, as well as the adjustments you need to make to your behavior from one to another, as they are all different. Almost all of them have some type of Mamasan, a lady who recruits and supervises the ladies day to day. The better the Mamasan, the better the ladies will be, and the better the club will be. Make sure you are always extremely nice to the Mamasan; it's a sign of respect and it will go a long way towards helping you in her establishment.

- Many men will not negotiate terms with a lady until the following morning. I negotiate terms with a lady before I leave with her or just as we're leaving. The guys who save it for later either get a ridiculous price that they have no choice but to pay, or the gal says, "Up to you." I find this to be terribly annoying and it's really just a tactic they use to try and see if you're stupid enough to pay too much. If you go too low they wouldn't accept it anyway, or they would and they'd tell everyone at the bar that you're cheap the next day. So don't leave it for the next day, and don't get stuck in a "Up to you" situation. Clearly negotiate the terms

before the night really begins, and as long as you're both happy with the price you'll have a much better time, and so will she, knowing that there is no uncomfortable negotiation looming. I talk about this more throughout the book as it relates to different ladies of the night.

Lady Bars

From the previous chapter, we now know about the girls we're likely to find in a bar, so let's discuss the bars themselves and how to handle yourself in them.

Most of the "lady bars" are outdoors, or you can at least see into them. Good eyes will help you here, so bring your glasses if you have trouble seeing from a distance. When you're picking out a bar to go to, you want to make sure that there is least one girl at the bar who is up to your standards and who isn't already sitting with a man. Don't go to sit down until you have confirmed this. Too many times a man goes into the bar, takes a seat, and then searches for a woman up to his standards. By this time it's too late and a girl he doesn't like comes to talk to him. Now he's stuck buying drinks for himself and for a lady he doesn't like. He may even wind up going home with the lady even though he's not attracted to her, and he won't have a great night. The best-case scenario if you're stuck in this spot is to tell the lady after the first drink that you're going to meet a friend and that it was nice to meet her. Don't get pressured into spending time and money on a girl you don't like. As long as you pinpoint a girl you like before you sit, then you're ok to proceed. You want to make eye contact with the girl of your choice before you sit. As long as she gives you some sort of positive sign, such as a smile, then take a seat as close to her as possible and act like she's the only girl in the room. I know in a real bar you try to ignore a girl at first and pay attention to her friends to make her jealous… This is not a real bar with real single women; you should not try and play it super cool. You should make it obvious to everyone that you intend to talk to and buy drinks only for the one lady, and you have no desire to talk to or even acknowledge any other women. In doing so you will prevent desperate and annoying bar girls from trying to compete with the woman you're talking to. The girls at a bar are jealous and they want money. If you don't make it clear that you're with the one woman, many of them will try and get you to buy them drinks, and it's just annoying. Even if you make it obvious, you can't stop the occasional lady from rudely interrupting the conversation you are having with your new friend and asking you for a drink. If you follow the rule above this won't happen a lot, but you'll experience it once in a while, no matter what. The best thing to do in that situation is to tell the annoying girl, "I'm sorry but I really like your friend here and I'll only be buying drinks for her tonight because I'm a one-woman-only kind of guy." Then quickly turn your attention back to your lady and forget the annoying girl ever existed.

So let's recap this information. We are careful about where we go, making sure to only go into a bar where we have confirmed an attractive lady is by herself, and only after she has confirmed that you are welcome with some sort of positive gesture. From there we confidently and deliberately go to her, sit, begin to talk and buy a round of drinks only for you and her. We don't pay any attention to any other women, and we don't let them con us into getting them drinks. Just to add a note to the "welcome confirmation" by the lady… If, when you start looking at her, she does not give you a smile but puts her head down and acts cold, it's obvious that she's not into you, or it's even possible she has a customer in the bathroom or on his way. Move on if this happens; she's not playing hard to get.

The time is also a factor and the earlier in the night the better chance you have of finding a pretty woman who is by herself. Going at the busy hours gives you every disadvantage and maximizes your own competition. Not as good as early in the night, but easily better than the middle of the night, is towards the very end, within an hour of when a bar closes. At this point the bar may have a lower bar fine rate, and the lady herself may charge a bit less seeing as though her window of opportunity is closing. I also like taking a lady with me as the bar closes because it means you are her last customer for the night. If you pay her for a short time she may elect to stay with you long-time if she likes you at no extra charge. There will be people who say you should pay her the full rate anyway, and this can be noted as being, **"Annoying Farang Fact #2."** Many ex-pats or seasoned Thai vets get upset if you don't pay a girl her full price for each minute you're with her. I suspect many of these same men also don't have so many opportunities to not pay full price and are jealous of this. But here is the right stance on the issue: always agree on a price for what you know you are totally sure will take place, and always agree on that before you are even near your place. Never give even 1 baht less than this agreed amount. If you paid for short time, and you guys are done with the deed and it seems like she's pretty tired and comfortable and not going anywhere anytime soon, you need to say something. If you don't say anything and you both wake up the next day and she asks for extra money for long-time, then it's on you to give it to her, and the annoying farang are right about that. But, you should say, "Listen, I only paid you for short time. I'm not paying for long-time tonight. Now, I had a really good time with you and I like you and I feel comfortable with you… so you're more than welcome to stay here for the night if you like. But I only paid for short time, so if you stay here for the night you'll be doing it for free." At this point if the lady does like you, she'll probably stay for free because she knows she'll get a superior night of sleep in your bed with some cold air, compared to her other option which is a hot room with two of her friends on her bed. In the morning, be sure to buy her breakfast and to pay for her transportation home; as inexpensive as these gestures are they go a long way to making the girl feel as if she is being treated well. And if you begin to see a girl multiple times or regularly, you can feel free to negotiate fees with her. I once asked a girl, would you rather see me four times a month at 1,000 baht per night or eight times a month at 700 baht per night. She said, of course 700 baht per night. That negotiation made me feel more comfortable about seeing her more often because I knew she was giving me a little bit of a break, and she appreciated the guaranteed business so it was a nice little arrangement. The bottom line here is that as long as the terms are clear, you don't have to pay a lady's top dollar every minute you see her indefinitely, and the farang that say otherwise are not even close to being as well-respected by the women as they think they are.

Back to the bar and there we are, making introductions and small chat with the girl we have targeted, confidently making sure she knows she is the only girl in the room as far as you're concerned. You have already impressed the girl at this point and she already feels excited that she may be in store for a more fun night than usual. It's important to continually smile. Smiling goes a long way towards making Thai women feel comfortable, because their pet peeve is usually "being too serious."

After you have made general introductions and bought the girl a drink, the girl is trained to "get to know you." This process is important to her; she continues to bait you into becoming a customer for the night while she gets paid for each drink you buy her, and she gets to size you up to see if you have value as a "more than one night customer," which is always in the back of her mind.

When she asks, "Is this your first time in Thailand?" Your answer is no, even if it is not true. If they get a sense that you are "fresh blood," they think they've hit the jackpot with you and there are no advantages for you that come as a result.

When she asks, "What you do for work?" I find the best answer is, "No, I'm finished with work." This is not a guess either; I have done more than enough experiments with all possible answers to see that by far the best reaction comes from saying that you no longer work, because you no longer need to work. And this answer is the best regardless of your age. They can only dream of not needing to work; it barely computes in their brain that its possible. You clearly have all of the freedom and flexibility in your life that you need, because you are traveling and they know that you don't have a job to report back to. You immediately become "long-term material" for them and they will treat you better for the rest of the night and beyond with more long-term goals in mind. You're not saying you're rich, which makes them want to get what they can out of you; you're saying that you have complete freedom in your life, which makes them want to enjoy that status with you. It never comes back to bite you in the ass either, even if you mistakenly fall in love with one of these girls. You can use it as an excuse not to buy her things she asks for by saying, "Hey babe, I don't have an income and I'm on a fixed budget for the rest of my life. It's a great way to live but there isn't a lot of extra room for things like jewelry or to buy your brother a motorbike." And if she eventually needs to know that you are employed, you just say you got bored and needed to start working again for your sanity.

So after the basic chit chat, its time to start making your exit. Why stay in the bar where she has to watch how she acts around people she sees every day, and while you pay extra for her "lady drinks"?

If it's early enough in the evening you can tell her you'd like to go out to dinner, or possibly another bar or disco. If she's interested in a big night out like this you should ask her what the bar fine is and what her rate is for long-time. Otherwise if you just want to take her back to your room for short- or long-time, that's fine too: just ask for the fees, and as long as they're not out of line with what they should be, you confirm and pay the bar fine and your tab. Once in a while, if you haven't made it clear that you know what you're doing, she may set an absurd price if she thinks she'll get it. Maybe she says 2,500 or 3,000 for long-time when it should be half of that. You should just smile and laugh a bit and say, "No, No... this isn't my first time." From there she should adjust her price back to reality, and if she doesn't then you are being looked at as a sucker and you should just find another lady that would be happy to have you for the correct price. Some people might say, "Who cares about an extra 1,000 baht?" But it's not about that, it's about the fact that this girl is charging you more than she would charge nearly every other guy. She doesn't charge you more if she likes you more! She charges you more because you've come across as a sucker. If she doesn't quickly adjust her price then it's a lost cause and the damage has been done. Whatever you do, don't negotiate after the deed is done. Then she can set whatever price she likes and you have no choice but to pay. You're not looking for problems, but you might have one if you hit this situation. So just to reiterate something I say many times: always make the terms clear BEFORE anything. You never go wrong with that strategy. The instructions for how to handle yourself once you have left her bar are in the next chapter.

One other topic is trying to get out of the bar fine. This can be done towards the end of the night by arranging to meet the lady you were talking to at a particular place, perhaps somewhere easy to find. I would never bring this up with a lady because it sounds extremely cheap and disrespectful, but some ladies will bring it up to you. It's a sales tactic for them; they use it to close you. They give you a "discount" without making a baht less for themselves at the end of the night. If the lady brings it up then I have nothing against it myself. But if the Mamasan lowers the bar fine at the end of the night, I'd just give it to her regardless, so you are welcome back anytime.

High-end Gogos

The high end Gogos usually have the prettiest ladies and the most expensive prices. You may find that some of them have nicer decor and possibly some interesting coordinated dance shows. These places are usually pretty crowded, especially by 11pm, and the environment might be a little more uptight. I don't recommend going to these places unless you are just looking for a great looking lady for the night and you are willing to pay upwards of 3,300 to 4,000 for long-time between the bar fine and the lady's fee. I do recommend that you go long-time with these girls. Short-time with a bar girl can work really well, and you're not overly rushed and it's cheap. But short-time and long-time in one of these places usually isn't much of a difference in price. If you're already spending 3,000, you might as well spend 4,000. A lot of the ladies at these places almost seem to get insulted if you don't want them for long-time. I don't let that get in the way of my decisions though, as sometimes I just have some place to be in a couple of hours and can't stay with her for the night even if I wanted to. If you do short time with them though, they're known to leave abruptly. They give you a fair amount of time, but when it's done, it's done and they're gone in a flash, usually back to the club to see if they can get a long-time "John" for the night. The music is usually loud at these clubs and you have a lot of competition because the farang there have most likely come prepared to spend some money.

So because of the competition, the prices, and the atmosphere, this place isn't ideal for drinking with your guy friends or trying to have a wild time with a bunch of girls. It's only about finding the lady you like and getting her out of there as quickly as you can. You might not find it particularly easy to talk to any girl you want, and once you do the loud dance music will make it difficult to have any type of meaningful conversation. This is ok though; you're not there for winning personalities.

Make sure you get to these places shortly after they open so you have your pick. Once you have identified the girl you would like to talk to, you can do one of a few things:

1) If she has a number, you can tell it to one of the hostesses and she'll send her over. Some of these clubs don't even use the number system and sometimes the hostesses don't interact much with the girls, so this may or may not be an option.
2) You can make some real eye-contact with her and insinuate that you'd like her to come over to you when she gets a chance. This may or may not work because she might be already preoccupied with another man. Yet another reason to get there early.
3) My personal favorite move is to go up to her, give her 100 baht and tell her she should come and have a drink with you when she gets a chance. If the hostesses are active in the club, you can have them give the 100 baht for you.

Unlike in the bars, you can play it cool in a high-end Gogo, and not be so deliberate about staring at the girl you like. She may not even like to be directly stared at while she dances for any long periods of time. Give her 100 baht or even 200 baht and she'll come over to you for a drink; she basically has to. I have genuinely enjoyed some conversations I've had with ladies at bars; many of them make me laugh and are very interesting, but not so much in the high-end GoGo's. The conversation is more about protocol than anything else. Humor her, but by the time her drink is almost done you should start talking about getting out of there for the night, and you can ask her if she'd like to come with you and what the rates are. I always want to make a good impression on every girl, so I put some effort into this each time. It's not that I don't care about the impression I can make on one of these high-priced hotties, it's that there is only so much I can accomplish in the loud and crowded club. Once I get them out of the club then I really turn the charm on, but the next chapter in the book delves into how to handle yourself once you leave with a special lady of the night.

Low-end Gogo's

In this situation, low-end does not necessarily mean inferior, it just means lower-priced and more relaxed. The girls on average will not be as pretty as the ones discussed above, but you'll probably have more of a fun time at this kind of establishment, especially if you're with a friend or a girlfriend. These places are actually excellent for when you have a girl with you who seems to be up for anything. A group of guys can also set their own tone and get a bit more rowdy here than they can in a higher-end establishment. There certainly is a place for them in your vacation or monthly routine.

There are a ton of these places, probably ten times more than the higher-end ones. It's hard to tell which has decent-looking girls. Sometimes you get to peek inside if the door opens; if that's the case make the most of your quick shot and try to size it up for yourself. You can generally look around online to see rankings of places, but it's more of a crap shoot then these sites make it out to be. The turnover in these places is extremely high. They can have a totally different lineup within a month, depending on a few factors. If they're not bringing in the guys, pretty girls are going to head elsewhere, and then the club can be in trouble, at least for a bit and until they regroup. Sometimes girls get bar-fined for a few nights by a customer, and some get taken very early in the night. You can be at a Gogo that has five pretty girls employed, but maybe by midnight all of them are gone. During the week and off the peak busy season you have a good shot at finding a cute girl or two at most places.

Going Gogo hopping is fine and since the prices of drinks aren't sky-high you can go to a few places without spending big money, and by doing this you widen the total number of girls you can choose from over the course of the night. About the only drawback of this is that you have to have at least one drink in each place you go to, and you may start to get drunk. These make for some fun nights, but just make sure you're not driving home.

Certainly at these places you can entertain multiple girls at your table, and if you're feeling really wild you can break a thousand into 20s and shower the stage with baht. Bar fines can go down to 300 at these places after 1am, so that's something to think about. Rates are just a bit higher for the girls than at the bars, which are easily worth it since you get to see exactly what you're paying for. At some of these clubs you can find some really pretty and fun girls; it won't happen every night out, but it happens plenty. All in all, such Gogos may be the most fun and versatile places to go to.

It's also easy enough to vacate with the girl of your choice. Unlike in the higher-end and overly crowded Gogos, you might not be in such a rush to leave, and it's not like the prices are sky-high on drinks. You're still probably not going to have wonderful conversations, and if you hang around for a while, the girl or girls you're spending time with will have to dance on stage at times.

So whether you want a really wild time, or you're not in the mood for a place with an attitude, and you don't mind going home with a 7, the typical Thai Gogo is for you.

Discos

Some guys thrive in the dance clubs and others feel out of place. I think they're an important piece to the puzzle though, because they offer you late night access to women and booze, and there is no bar fine for the ladies. As I discussed before, I tend to think highly of the girls you'll find at the discos in comparison with other types of working girls. Certainly if you're out for the true girlfriend experience, a night at a disco is your best option because the process to meet a girl there is the most natural. Actually it's not really different from meeting a girl at a club back home, other than it being much easier, and the 1,000 baht you slip her at some point in the night.

Discos in Thailand tend to be free to enter, and almost all of them have freelance girls in their establishments. You can go into one by yourself and you'll be able to meet a girl, dance with that girl, enjoy a few drinks with that girl and taker her home. You can skip most of the drinks and the dancing if you prefer to do so. I find that, like most young girls, Thai women do like to dance. I can't say they're great dancers, but I think that is mostly because they don't have access to dance classes and they grow up on different music from what's played at the clubs.

Discos are also fine to go to with your friends, but I suggest buying a bottle if you are there with at least one guy friend. Bottle service back home is an expensive proposition, but luckily in Thailand it can be the economical choice. Bottles of cheaper whisky may be around 2,000 baht depending on the class of the disco. This has to wind up being cheaper than individually buying the same amount of drinks that come in a bottle, factoring in tips. And as in any country, having a bottle secures you a table, a little privacy, and certainly won't hurt with the ladies. If you're single there's really no need, but if you're in the mood to splurge, getting a bottle and a table at a posh night club will almost guarantee that you will be hanging out with multiple girls at a time, something most men will enjoy. Also, back home if you don't buy a bottle you get no table; however, if there are free tables at a slew of clubs in Thailand, you can sit at one with something like a two- to four-drink minimum, which is great.

Bottle or not, asking a girl if she would like a drink is probably a good start with a disco freelancer. It might not be the move of choice back home, but it gets the job done in Thailand. If a girl lets you buy her a drink, it's likely that she'll go home with you if you want. It should be apparent whether or not a woman is a freelancer, but if she's not then it's a whole different ball game and it may be an uphill battle. If a woman is with a group of Thai people including some Thai men, possibly at a table with a bottle of whisky, you're probably not looking at a "lady of the evening." You certainly don't want to make the mistake of treating a non-freelancer like a freelancer. It could cause trouble if she is there with a male Thai friend or especially if she's there with her Thai boyfriend. Just be cautious. If a girl is there by herself, its certain that she's "working", and if she's there with only other Thai ladies, then there's no worst-case scenario, even if she isn't a pay-for-play specialist. In Bangkok you will find some non-freelancers who are at a club just looking for a good time, and some of them might be looking to get swept off their feet by a Western man. Use your best judgment, and again as long as you are respectful, and she's not with Thai men, then you'll be fine. Make sure "How much?" is NOT your ice breaker!

If you give a girl "the look", she might come up to you, and that makes things easy. As always, make sure you are all smiles and you offer her a drink immediately. Tip your bar tender to make a good impression and so that you don't have to wait forever the next time you want a drink. If you take good care of the bar tenders at discos, they usually take good care of you.

I can't think of too many sub-par nights I've had at Thai night clubs. I usually get what I want there, even if it's just a place to bring a bar girl for an hour before we go home. Occasionally you might find a lack of real "talent", especially if you go late night, but at a minimum you should find a cute enough girl. There is a lot of flexibility and choice at the clubs. At the bars you feel compelled to stay with the same girl you initially buy drinks for, and the bar fine looms. At a disco, you can talk to as many women as you like. When you're ready to go home, you can be natural and ask her if she's ready to leave. I recommend negotiating the terms of the night just outside of the disco once you have exited. There at least you'll both have privacy and it won't ruin the mood. You'll also be within distance should you not be able to reach an agreement. Most of the time you will reach an agreement; she has no real leverage to take advantage of you with an outrageous price if you're standing within spitting distance of a club filled with 100 other ladies. Leave the negotiating till you're in your room and you're likely to ruin the mood and to get a higher price.

Soapy Massage

Bliss, Heaven, and Happiness: these are words used to accurately describe the soapy massage experience. They're also probably the names of some soapy massage parlors, but that's beside the point. Truly a one of a kind Asian experience, this should be on your list of things to do.

Identifying a soapy massage parlor shouldn't be difficult; unlike most massage parlors there is usually a "fish bowl," or cluster of available specialists sitting in the welcome room often with numbers. Small and large places will have some sort of host who tells you the prices and might offer to sell you a beer. You don't have to be in a rush, so sit down and have a cold one while you let the girls woo you for their attention. Some of the girls may have different colored numbers, with one color representing a higher price. The difference in price is usually minimal so don't let this phase you. Pick the attractive girl who looks like she's not uptight and who has made it clear to you that she would like you to pick her. Also, don't discriminate against the girls with the "cheaper color." These places have their own reasons for their colors and a lot of them aren't good reasons. I have seen prettier and nicer girls with the cheaper color at times. The owner might not have the same taste as you do. Many Western men like dark skin, but Thai men much prefer pale skin. You might get a bargain simply because a woman has a tan.

Once you pick your lady, your work is done. Expect to come out of the parlor nearly two hours later with an ear-to-ear grin on your face. You will have the most incredible time of your life in there as long as you're with a giving woman. There's water, baths, soap, and a lot of body parts interacting in all sorts of crazy ways. It's like a roller coaster! They're always full service, so you get a little bit of everything you could ever want. They usually range in price, depending on the class of the establishment and the talent, from $1,600 to $2,300. A tip of 300 baht to the lady will be a nice gesture as well but is not mandatory.

If you're on vacation you might want two soapy massages, and if you live in Thailand it will most likely be a monthly or even bi-weekly event. I couldn't even imagine how much they would charge back home for a service like this.

Happy-Ending Massage

Not all massage parlors in Thailand offer special services, but you should be able to spot the ones that do because the women will be wearing "slutty clothes" as opposed to "masseuse clothes." You'll also get to pick very quickly from a handful of girls. It's not like a soapy massage where you can take a while to pick the lady; you need to make a decision almost immediately. Nothing is usually mentioned up-front other than you wanting the full body oil massage. The establishment charges you about 300 baht for this. Depending on where in Thailand you are, some of these girls who are willing to give happy-ending massages probably come across some people who don't want this service. Let her know you're not that guy by disrobing completely with no questions asked once you're in the room. Don't be shy; they've massaged naked guys who look worse than you—guaranteed. As long as you smell nice, you're good to go. And don't feel awkward about anything while you're in there. You're there to enjoy yourself; if that means that you're at full attention at times, then so be it. You're in there really to get some combination of a decent massage and a happy ending, and this can be confusing to your anatomy at times. Again, just go with it and enjoy yourself.

At a certain point she'll ask you if you want a special massage. Some type of negotiation will ensue. For either a great "rub and tug" or full oral, you're probably looking at 500 baht to slightly more; this is in addition to the 300 baht to the house. If there is no sex then just make sure you don't spend more than 1,000 in total. I've heard of the girls saying, oh its 1,000 and then the man finds out later she meant 1,000 in addition to the 300 for the house, and then the man feels compelled to tip and all of a sudden its practically the same price as a soapy. This is not the same as a soapy; it's not as good and it's not as expensive. If she says 500 and she's nice, then you give her the extra 200 change from the 1,000 baht.

If she never asks you for the special massage and you notice that there isn't much left of the hour then you may ask her what's going on. If she acts shocked that you'd ask her such a question, don't get embarrassed, that's part of the hustle. You see even the staff at the most legitimate of massage parlors in Thailand, who would never offer special services, have indeed been asked for them. You haven't made the mistake of going to one of these places, so in the worst case you're at a place that at least resembles a "happy ending" massage parlor. So if she acts like she's never been asked that question before, it is precisely that, an act. You may be at a place that doesn't give special services; but they're well aware you probably expect it; they know you wouldn't have come in without expecting it in many situations. They need the business and that's that. Or you might be with a girl who just doesn't want to give it to you for whatever reason at that moment. If this happens there isn't much you can do. You won't be the first guy to come out of one of these shops and walk immediately into another, more "sure thing" place, and you won't be the last.

Chapter 4: PLACES TO AVOID

Bars and massage parlors that don't offer special services

Not every bar or massage parlor exists to help pair you with a woman you can get your rocks off with.

I should be clear: there are great bars and massage parlors that don't offer any ladies in that way and I frequent places like this for a nice change of pace. When I say to avoid them, I only mean if you're "on the hunt." There are a lot of very nice Irish pubs in the major cities of Thailand. These places do not have bar fines and you are not supposed to hit on their staff. If you want a vacation from your vacation, or you want to be in a place that reminds you of home if you're here for a long stretch, the Irish pub can be a great place to watch a sporting event and enjoy some imported beer. You can bring your lady there; just make sure she's dressed appropriately.

As far as the massage parlors go, I mentioned in the last chapter that if the women are wearing a massage outfit that is in no way suggestive or slutty, the chances are good that they offer no special services. These places do sometimes offer very highly skilled masseuses who give one of the world's best and cheapest massages, but there will be no hanky-panky. There is certainly a place for this between wild nights out or a few times per month if you live here. The caution is just not to expect or even try to solicit special favors at such a place.

How to spot a lady boy

People come to Thailand with all different types of desires and tastes. If you are into lady boys then you probably won't have a difficult time spotting them, and you can read about them in Chapter 20. This section is specifically for men who are not at all interested in them and who want to make sure they avoid them. This can be easier said than done unfortunately, especially if you're inebriated.

There are more trans-gender people in Thailand than you are used to seeing back home. The speculation is that any Thai man who is even remotely gay can enjoy an easy enough career by becoming a lady boy in Thailand as opposed to living a difficult life doing hard labor for very little money. These men want to strike the same gold that some ladies do. It can work that way, but often times it doesn't and the lady boys can live a difficult life here. Most of them do have trouble meeting clients and making money, and when they get older it's not a good situation. Even if you're repulsed by the thought of being with a lady boy, you should still respect them like any other strangers, and understand their plight.

The interesting phenomenon to me is that lady boys do get at least enough business to survive even though there are so many of them. True-blue gay men are likely to go to a "gay" establishment with gay Thai men who are not lady boys. This means that there are a decent number of men who most likely are totally straight in their day-to-day lives back home, but are not quite totally straight when they are in Thailand. If this wasn't the case then there would be no lady boys working, right? Yes there are some lady boys who can fool someone into thinking they are a real lady, and I'll address that shortly; but easily 95 per cent would not be mistaken for a lady under any circumstance and yet they get customers. If you have any temptation to see what it's like, you can do that here and you can do it discreetly if you wish. If you, like me, have no desire to experiment even one time for even one minute, then you need to be somewhat cautious.

Since Thai men are built slender and short, they can transform themselves to look like a lady if they have the right features and the right surgeries. I was told numerous times that some of the most beautiful women in the pay-for-play industry are not women at all, specifically in Bangkok. I think I have a pretty good eye for spotting them, easily better than most, and yet I've been fooled before, fortunately, never past a certain point. However, I have mistaken two lady boys for real ladies and bought both of them a drink. Luckily it didn't go past that point before I realized that something was off, but it easily could have if I'd been drunk. Again, if a man is built small to begin with, and has some female characteristics and invests money and time into the transformation, it might start to get very difficult to tell the difference. Additionally, they might actually have certain advantages over a lady, such as an athletic build and a nice boob job. Usually the boob job is a dead give-away, but after a lot of plastic surgery and even years of a hormone cocktail combination or medication, it gets difficult. This I can guarantee you: there are at least a few dozen lady boys in Bangkok who would be mistaken for beautiful women almost every time. So, here are the things you should look out for if you're trying to avoid a lady boy:

1) **A cock.** If they have a cock, they're probably not a real lady. Sorry, but I couldn't avoid the setup here for a vulgar and stupid joke. But actually it is worth mentioning that some of the lady boys have had the surgery to remove their package, while others haven't. Many of them want it but can't afford it. The ones in Bangkok that I have warned you about will have had the surgery. Otherwise, don't accept oral or kiss a girl you're not totally sure about unless you make sure there is nothing between their legs.

2) **Your instinct.** Look, I know what to look for; for some strange reason I'm actually quite well versed in plastic surgery, and as I said, I bought two lady boys drinks. Of course this was bound to happen over the course of years, but both times what saved me was my instinct. They both passed all of the physical tests, A+ even, but something told me inside that something didn't seem right. And if you ever get this feeling you're probably not wrong.

3) **Boob Job.** Thailand isn't Malibu; women don't get boob jobs unless a long-term boyfriend coerces them into it, and there are actually some expensive Gogos that encourage the women to. But I'd say the average Western girl is ten times more likely to have a boob job. So if a girl clearly has fake cans it doesn't mean she's a lady boy, but it means you should double and triple check. Most lady boys do have them, so this is usually the first red flag.

4) **Hands.** Men and women don't have the same type of hands, and Thai boys usually do hard labor from when they're young. So take a good look. Back home the Adam's apple is more of a dead giveaway than anything else, but Thai men don't have the protruding Adam's

apple so much, and it can even be shaved down these days. There is no surgery, to my knowledge, to make a hand smaller and more feminine.

5) **Voice.** A really slick lady boy who has made a career of being all-woman in the eyes of their customers has spent some time working on his/her voice. There is only so much they can do however, because Thai men have just as deep a voice as any others. I like to use the "Michael Jackson test" for this. If their voice sounds like Michael Jackson's and it always seems like they're trying to keep the decibels at minimum, it's probably a lady boy.

6) **The full Monty.** By this point you've already gone way too far, so this is kind of like the eject button on a fighter jet. You may live if you eject from a fighter jet that's headed for the ground, but you probably will never be the same after. And so it can be if you figure out that a lady's vagina does not look the way it should, or worse yet, does not *feel* the way it should. If you have to check to make sure that you're in the right hole, you're in trouble because she's not in the right line of work to be that tight by nature. Why am I telling you this? Would it have been better to have unknowingly made the mistake? Probably, but we don't want this to turn into "The Crying Game", and you absolutely would rather know immediately than know after any length of time has gone by, right?

Russian Gogo's

Let's start out with: **Annoying Farang fact #3.** A lot of veterans, who were possibly not a big hit back home with the white ladies, now seem to have an axe to grind with any white women. So if you tell a few guys, "Hey I need a white girl tonight," it's possible that you'll get an earful. They might go on a rant about how you shouldn't come to Thailand if you want a white woman and how white woman are big and ugly. This is totally ridiculous. As with any race, there are some unbelievable-looking white women. And as most men do, sometimes you want a little variety, or you might miss the occasional piece of white meat.

Now if you're here for a week and it's your first time in Thailand, these annoying farang have a point, and I suggest you stick to Thai women because it's just easier and cheaper that way. But if you live here or you're here for an extended period of time, you have every right to satisfy an urge for anything that pleases you. If this is the case, you don't have a ton of options, but there are some white women available in Bangkok and in Pattaya. Whatever you do, just don't make the mistake of trying to find one at a "European Gogo." Fortunately there aren't many of these in Thailand, but there's a couple, and many guys fall victim to these places.

From what I understand there is a certain type of person who does not have buyer's remorse when leaving one of these establishments: rich Asian/Arab Men (mostly rich Asian men). We know there are some very wealthy men from places like Tokyo, Shanghai, and Dubai, and it isn't every day that they have a buffet of beautiful white women to enjoy themselves with. These men can afford to spend 100,000 baht and not get laid, and still not blink an eye. Most people reading this probably don't feel the same way and so I suggest you don't go to these places.

In the interest of this book I have been to all of them, and the best time I had there was when I spent 30,000 baht and, you guessed it... I did not go home with anyone. I did spend a lot of time with some gorgeous women and I had a lot of fun, but I had myself a case of buyer's remorse. The other times I didn't have a good time at all and I spent maybe 3,000 to 6,000 baht.

The drinks are Moscow prices (that means high), and every girl will keep expecting you to give her 100 baht every time she goes near you. Then if you talk to one she'll have you buy her tea, chocolate, and a flower which will total about 4,000 baht. And they'll re-sell that flower after you leave to the next guy. They do have bar fines, but they're insane, maybe 6,000 to 9,000, and that again is simply a bar fine. Some of the girls won't even talk about sex because it's off the table, and I suppose the ones that will talk about it will have Moscow prices (that means *really* high). Are the girls gorgeous? Yes, some of them are like out of a magazine, but they're an illusion, so it doesn't matter. There are less attractive but REAL Eastern European women available at typical back-home prices in Bangkok and in Pattaya. Some of the less attractive ones at the European Gogo's might be interested at a price that isn't off the wall, but you'll spend thousands of baht just by walking in to the Gogo, so it's not worth it.

There is sort of an underground escort group of Russian women available in Pattaya and Bangkok, but it's not easy to find them. You can find some escort sites in Bangkok with a few Google searches, again just be prepared to spend. In Pattaya you don't want to go crazy asking around, but if you talk to the right concierge in a hotel or you go to some of the Walking Street discos (usually by the pier), you'll be able to find them. I find the whole thing feels almost as if it was back home so I avoid it, and my general suggestion is that you do as well. But I'm trying to be thorough here, so I put it all on the table.

Do not assume that Russian girls at a disco are automatically freelancers. Some of them in Bangkok and Pattaya are, but some of them are with their husbands. You do not want to get on the wrong side of a Russian woman here, or her boyfriend or employer. The Russian prostitutes in Thailand usually go with rich Asian men, Arabs, and other Russians. Of course there are exceptions, and once in a blue, a girl at a Gogo solicits a Western man and all goes well. It's rare, and unlikely to happen to you unless you're out all of the time. If you see two white Eastern European women by themselves at the disco, and you're sure their husbands aren't just in the bathroom, then you can say hello and see what happens. They don't speak much English, but if they're working, you will be able to figure it out. Prices usually run from 3,000 to 5,000 for the night, but during slow season they are known to go more in a range of 2,000 to 3,000 unless they're a knockout.

So the annoying farang are wrong to criticize you for wanting a white woman, but they have a point about it being a little more work and money than it might be worth. To each their own.

Karaoke bars

Karaoke bars in Thailand have become somewhat popular amongst Thai people as a fun thing to do on a weekend. If you have a girlfriend and she wants to go, then by all means go with her and you guys will enjoy each other, and they may even have a Beatles song or two in their catalogue for you to sing if you so desire. But don't go to a karaoke bar alone or in search of a lady.

Karaoke bars do usually have some type of pay-for-play staff available, but if they go home with a customer it's usually a Thai man and it's usually when the place closes. These places just aren't geared for farang in anyway. If they're having a slow night, they may invite you in from the street and say they have ladies for you. Just say "No Thank You" and go elsewhere. You are so much better off in any of the other types of establishments discussed above. If for no better reason, there have been many reports of farang men having bad experiences at these places. Giving them the benefit of the doubt, let's just say the Western men were surprised and shocked when they got their final bill. We've heard many of these stories, especially in Bangkok where they take you to "another room." If it's just one big room and it's just a normal karaoke bar, you don't have to worry about anything bad happening; it's just not a great place to meet women.

Chapter 5: YOU MADE A NEW FRIEND... WHAT NOW?

This may be the most important chapter of the book, but it's often overlooked because most men

just assume that they can do no wrong with a Thai girl they're paying. I understand this is how it should be. You're paying for a Thai girl's time so it should be about you and your enjoyment, and there should be no thought process. But just how much fun you have with a particular playmate will often depend on how you handle yourself with her from the first impression and going forward. Are you going to be a chore or a job to this girl, OR is she going to fall in love with you on the spot and hope that you change her life? Certainly you have the control for either scenario in most situations as long as you know what to do.

Demeanor, Mood, and Attitude: Plan Of Action

In trying to set the tone for a night out with a Thai lady of the evening, it's important to set forth your goals. If you're just trying to get laid with minimal effort and for minimal cash without a care in the world about much else, you won't need much help to make that happen. You leave the bar, you go back to your place and you let nature take its course. Perhaps we've all felt this way at times, when we just want a quick fix and we're not looking for anything earth-shattering. It'll scratch the itch, but there is a limit to the level of satisfaction you'll feel with that type of minimal effort. And while many men might talk about how they're just a "hunter" out to get as much flesh as they can, in reality most of them seek more. Even if we know that we will probably never see the Thai lady after the night is officially over, we can get out of the experience what we put into it. If we make some sort of connection with the lady, of course every moment of the night from that point on will be more significant and more special. When you make her forget that she's "working", and when you forget that "you're a customer" for stretches of the night because it's that comfortable and you're having that much fun, you're usually in for a hell of a night. So here is a list of what we may desire in a night out with a bar lady when we aren't simply "hunting for flesh":

-To have a great time the entire time

-To do some things those aren't as fun to do by yourself, and I 'm talking more in terms of "nice dinner" than I am in terms of bedroom, initially anyway.

-To make the girl feel comfortable

-To stand out from the typical experience she has

-To have great sex

-To have such a good time that by the end you both have an interest in doing it again, and not just because you're getting your rocks off, and not just because she would get more money.

If you and the lady are to have a good time the entire time, it's important to make a good REAL first impression. You see, the impression you make at the bar or at the Gogo is important, and we've already discussed what that entails, but you can only get so far while you're both surrounded by her boss and all of her friends and co-workers. As soon as you leave with her, that's when it's critical to let her know that tonight is going to be different, and her night of "working" has officially ended. As long as we have the "terms of the night", it's time to set a little bit of an agenda. It's true that many bar girls would prefer a night of sleep to a crazy night out, but you can both sleep in the following night if all goes well on night-one. Certainly, going straight back to your place isn't going to be magical for either one of you;

therefore, soon after leaving the establishment I usually find a place to talk with her and I see what she's up for.

"Are you hungry?" Many bar girls might feel compelled to say no to this question, so I start by telling them that I'm really hungry and I tell them I'll take them to any place they'd like to go to get something to eat. Even if it's late there's always something open with some good food. If she's too shy to order in front of you, tell her to order you something good and when it's on the table she won't be able to resist. Either way you should make her feel that this isn't some kind of fine-dining experience. You want her to feel comfortable enough to pig out in front of you. Tell her to get into it! *"Don't be shy now; that food isn't going to eat itself."* I've been here long enough to know that if a Thai girl gets to pig out on the food of her choice without feeling awkward, she's going to be in a good mood. A couple of drinks won't hurt either. She might not be a drinker, but as long as she's had a couple of drinks she'll be more likely to relax with you. The key is to keep it light, to keep it

relaxed, and to joke around. It'll be easy enough to joke around since one of you doesn't speak great English and one of you doesn't speak even half-way decent Thai. You get a kick out of the way she tries to speak English and she'll laugh every time you try to speak Thai and just completely butcher it

I find Thai women to be very easy to talk to, no matter what their level of English is. Think about it, how hard could it be to find things to talk about when you both live in different worlds? She can teach you things about her culture and you can teach her thing about yours. Just make sure you're pointing out differences that aren't a slight to Thailand. For instance, you may talk about how damn expensive things are at home or how people go crazy for good Thai food in your country because it's so hard to come by. That's fine. Talking about how superior the education system is in the West... not good conversation material there. Before I knew any Thai I took out a couple of girls who didn't know any English. I was literally drawing pictures for them and they were doing the same. It was like playing charades. But the girls totally appreciated the effort, and after a couple of drinks each, it was actually a blast to play drunken charades! I now have an application on my cell phone, "Google Translate", that lets me talk into it and it translates everything into Thai. You might not be able to get this squared away on vacation, but if you're here for a while its worth having some type of data plan just to have the mobile translator.

While you're finishing up a fun meal or round of drinks, it's time to ask her about what she'd like to do next. This is a three-step process: meal/booze, something interesting, and then back to your place. For the after-dinner place, I suggest asking her if she'd rather go to a disco for a half-hour or take a nice short walk with you (if you're near a beach, that's a great place for a walk). I stress

making sure she knows you don't intend to stay out all night with her, because she might worry about this, so let her know that, either way, it'll be relatively short. Try to find a way to buy her something silly, like a flower or a stuffed animal, or a picture from one of the Polaroid vendors. She'll appreciate that you're trying and she also likes that you are helping struggling street vendors. Thai people like when you take care of other Thai people, and there's no shame in that.

So after a solid round of dancing or a nice stroll in some place beautiful (or in Bangkok's case, some place interesting), it's time to take things back to where the magic happens. You've been a gentleman, you've been confident, and you've shown her a great time. She knows you're not a sucker, but she knows you're certainly not cheap, and she finds you interesting and fun. This bodes well for the rest of the night.

Even the most seasoned Thai bar girl might actually be a little intimidated by you, especially if she likes you. When you get back to your place, find something to do for about fifteen minutes. This is important. This isn't the movie *9 ½ Weeks*; she's not going to be ripping your clothes off in the elevator. You've done great work in making her feel comfortable for the whole night, and you don't want to ruin that because of a little "Uh-oh, now it's sex time" anxiety. Have her take a seat and take your laptop out. Show her something interesting, maybe some Google images of where you're from, or a YouTube video of something you talked about during the night. If there were any language problems and you weren't equipped on your mobile, Google Translate works wonders from your laptop. So give her some water, talk a bit more, show her some pictures, and show her something funny. Anything that takes about fifteen minutes, and is sort of interesting or enjoyable, is perfect. A girl I was with who spoke almost no English was obsessed with "Paintbrush" on my laptop, and she spent thirty minutes drawing me love pictures.

So after you have managed to kill a little time at your apartment, now you can let the "moment" happen naturally, and it'll be so much more enjoyable and comfortable for her that way. In the midst of good conversation you can actually look at her with the dramatic-pause effect and get a solid kiss in there, whether it's your first of the night or not.

Thai girls find it necessary to shower before they hit the sheets. I wish Western women were equally hygienic. So she will have to take a shower and she'll want you to take one before any of the real fun starts. Most of the time, they'll make a move to shower alone, and then you'll do so after. I find this ruins some of the progress we've been making, so I almost always shower with the girl. Do whatever it takes to take a shower with her; this is so much fun and it'll keep the mood going. Some seasoned ex-pats might mistakenly tell you that most girls won't take a shower with you. I get them all to shower with me and they're not doing it as a chore or out of pity; they're doing it because we shared some moments during the night, including the one just before the shower, and if I ask them really sweetly if I can shower with them, they always say yes. The only reason they would say no is because they're embarrassed about their body (which even some hot girls are), and they'd rather you see them with the lights off. Strip down and say anything stupid like, "Hey, no peaking." Your both probably buzzed, so it can't be too hard to make her laugh while you flap around naked telling her you'd like to give her a "tour of your shower" and a lesson on "how not to get burned or to fall in your particular shower." One time I was drunk enough to ask a girl to teach me how to take a shower, and it worked. She literally went along with the joke and taught me how to shower. I'm not sure I've ever said the same line twice, but you get the idea. I strip; I'm obviously not perfect and I make it pretty clear that I don't care that *they're* not perfect. I just make them laugh and within minutes there is some heavy groping going on in that shower. One thing is certain by the time we leave the shower… her breasts and my penis are the cleanest body parts in Asia.

So you're both in towels now; make sure to put the condom and the lubrication under the pillow. This isn't the Kama Sutra; I'm not going to teach you sex techniques. I just know that the more comfortable we both are, the better the sex usually is for both of us. Being comfortable with a woman you just met usually isn't easy, which is why I have outlined the step-by-step instructions for you on how to do just that with a bar girl. The rest is up to you; it's not as if certain styles between the sheets work better on Thai women than on other women. As we all know, every woman is different! Afterwards, ask if her if she wants to borrow a shirt, they usually do. You've done great work and you've had a great night, so it's time to get yourself some rest.

The average experience for a bar girl with a farang usually goes one of two possible ways. Either they meet a guy who just takes them back immediately after leaving the bar and wants to get right to the bedroom, which certainly won't leave a lasting impression on her; or, she meets a man who is smitten and can't stop complimenting her, and once he's had a few drinks he starts saying completely ridiculous things. In either of those situations, the girl never forgets she's working, and she either runs out of your place at the first chance she gets, or she tries to get as much money out of you as she can. The night I have outlined above sets you apart from the regular Joes out there. Just make sure you handle your alcohol. Pace yourself and follow the guide and she'll be more than happy to show you a great time.

Out of all of the nights I've had like the ideal one I described, I'd say I wake up before the girl does most of the time. Whenever I do I get her breakfast and I wake her up with a variation of breakfast in bed. Usually this nice gesture ensures a Round 2 of boot-knocking action.

All good things come to an end... or do they? You may be conflicted around noon the next day about what to do with this awesome lady. The sooner you end it the better, usually, but there are exceptions, and who can blame you for wanting to keep the party going, especially if you're on vacation and you think this girl is the bee's knees.

Throughout the book I talk about the prospects of short and long term relationships with bar girls. For this chapter, we're assuming you can make a decision on how you'd like to proceed with a girl once the line between day-one and day-two begins to blur. So there are three different scenarios, and here is how they unfold:

The End-game No. 1: Thank you, have a nice life.

I don't know all of the words to the song at the end of "Dirty Dancing," but I know it starts with, "I've had the time of my life." I should play that song every morning with a bar girl. The bottom line is, you're up, you're sober, and you don't feel like spending the rest of the afternoon with this girl, let alone another twenty-four hours. Last night was beautiful, but last night is over. You think she's a wonderful gal and you wish her all the best but you don't get the feeling that you'll be a "repeat customer" of hers anytime soon.

If you followed the steps above you also have a girl in front of you who may be hoping for a different outcome then she's about to get. These girls have all been "let go" before with a farang they wanted to spend more time with, so it's not as if you're going to break her heart, but she might be genuinely disappointed. I don't like to lead the girl on in these situations, but I like to be as polite as possible.

I tell her, "Ok, I have a little bit of work to do, why don't you get your things together and come over here and give me a big hug." Then I tell them to give me their phone number and I say maybe we'll hang out some time. And lastly I give them 100 baht for a ride home, and I specifically tell them that is for the ride home, so they know it's not some kind of BS tip. No tips; they got plenty. I paid them the amount we agreed on, I treated them to a whole night out, I was a perfect gentleman, and I got them breakfast and a ride home. The gravy train stops there.

If they ask me for my phone number, I tell them I'm getting a new sim card soon, but I'll call her if I can hang out. If she flat-out asks me, "Are you going to see me again, or do you want me to stay with you today?" I say, "I don't know but I'm going to try." Most of them have too much pride to beg, and as sad as they might be they'll give you a hug and leave knowing you won't call them again. It's strange that you have to pay her and yet she's sad about not being able to spend time with you, but that happens all of the time. Don't get me wrong, there will be plenty of girls who leave and show no apparent signs of sadness. They also realize that having a great night once with you was better than none at all. Once in a while you'll have a girl put on a show and she'll start crying and telling you about how much she hates working in the bar. This happens a lot more often if you spend a lot of time with them prior to your exit (which I'll get to in a bit), but if she's new to the scene and you give her the best night she's had in a long time, it's possible to see this after one night. She knows you're not a sucker, so this is probably because she likes you than rather than she's conning you, but always be on your guard. Either way, don't ever let a few tears influence any of your decisions with women; if it's that easy for them then God help us all! You just have to remind her that it was great, but that you have a life outside of Thailand and that she's a great lady and she's not going to have any problems meeting a better guy than you. And that's that.

The End-game No. 2: Thank you, maybe we can do this again some time.

This scenario is easy enough. You enjoyed your time with the lady and you're not against seeing her again, but the fireworks weren't going off to the point of you wanting to keep her with you without interruption. What makes this easy is that you don't care much either way and you don't need to

dance around the truth. When I'm in this position I give the girl my phone number and I tell her to call me in a week if she gets off work one day and would like to see me. By doing this I give both of us an extra incentive. It works out well for her if she has a night in the near future when she doesn't get a customer and/or she's lonely. In this case she can just give me a call and there's a chance she has a customer she can be comfortable with. My incentive is that she'll probably come directly to my apartment with no bar fines and no major work. I've already wined and dined her and there's an established chemistry so we might have a very good time staying in and watching TV and playing hide the salami. If she doesn't call, I'll live; if she calls and I'm with someone, I don't pick up. It's really a win-win situation for as long as you don't catch feelings for the girl.

The End-game No. 3: Thank you, stay for a while.

Annoying Farang Fact #4- Many veterans who don't have good experiences past one night with bar girls begin to think that it's impossible for anyone to have a good experience with a bar girl past one night. If we're talking in terms of weeks, I'd agree; but in terms of days I think it's very practical to have an amazing time with a bar girl without breaking the bank. You need to know when to call it quits though, and you need to have the strength to follow through with the end-game.

I discuss at length the long-term prospects of being with a bar girl in the next chapter, so for this chapter's sake let's just assume that you meet a girl you really want to keep spending time with and you are fully prepared to end it within one week's time. You bar-fined her the night before and there you are the next day through breakfast, so now it's time to take the steps necessary to try and talk her into staying with you for a bit without it costing more than it should. To reiterate a common theme in this book, we have no problem fairly compensating any woman for her time in this industry, but we never want to be taken advantage of, because that accomplishes nothing positive.

Depending on the venue she works in, she probably has to meet some type of quota with her Mamasan for revenue, through bar fines and drinks. If a girl spends a week with you, she will have some debt with her bar if she intends to keep working there. Most of the bars are smart enough to hold funds back for this very reason. If the girl just bails with no arrangement, she'll lose some money in most situations. So in any event when you ask a girl to stay with you for a few days or for a week, you have to find out what her bar will charge for the time, and then you'll also need to figure out a fair price for the lady's time. These prices vary widely, as do the opinions of veterans on how to handle it.

With girls from the Gogo's, they might owe their Mamasan 600 to 800 baht for each day they take off. They may also figure that each day they spend with you equates to about 2,500 out of their pocket that they would normally make in a night. Of course when they do this computing, they aren't factoring in their occasional bad night and how their real average is lower than that, but you're not going to audit her so take it with a grain of salt. She might expect to charge you a total of over 3,000 baht per day, maybe 20,000 for the week for her and the Gogo if she's a looker. A lot of guys will just ask her how much, then she'll quote high and the guy will say, "OK." Now the woman knows the man is incapable of saying no to her, so she'll take an "order the most expensive thing on the menu" approach with the man for the rest of their time together. You want to take a more pro-active approach. There is a way to negotiate with these women in a way where you don't come off cheap and you don't come off as a sucker. That is the sweet spot; the woman knows you have money, but that you don't waste it and you're not a pushover. She'll respect you more if you can achieve this balance. I usually offer a price before they give me a quote. I always go low with it, and they go higher , then we agree on something fair. This will get you a lower price than just flat-out asking her, "how much" every time.

You can start by saying, "Listen, that was a great time last night and we should keep it going. Why don't you let me **do you a favor** and cover your bar fines for a few nights so you can take some time off with me? If you took off a week, the club will charge you, what, 3,000 baht? "

She'll immediately correct you and tell you the real amount the Gogo will charge her might be 4,000 to 5,000 baht. At least by going low you get the real price. If you ask her, rather than suggesting that it's low, she'll probably quote you higher than it really is.

Next you say, "OK, so I need to pay your Gogo 4,000 baht, no problem, and I'll also give you 1,00 baht each day for you to pay your rent or send to your family… whatever you would like to do with it. And of course I'll take great care of you for the time we spend together; you won't spend a single baht with me and it'll beat dancing all night for a bunch of horny guys." A high-end dancer at a Gogo will not be happy with 1,000 baht per day, because she could make three times that every day. But, by now she knows that you're no pushover and you're wise to the scene. If she likes you even a little bit she's probably going to give you a fair quote with the next words out of her mouth, perhaps 1500 baht per day. This would now be a total of about 15,000 baht for her and the Gogo for the week. You weren't lying when you told her she'd have a better time with you than working at the Gogo every night, and surely you will be treating her to nice meals each day you're with her, possibly even a trip to some place nice. It's a good deal for her. Look, if you wind up spending slightly more with a really hot Gogo dancer, that's understandable. But by establishing that you're not just going to spend any wild amount of money she comes up with, and by taking the initiative with her, you won't be looked at as an ATM machine any longer, and she'll no you're a savvy guy.

TWO IMPORTANT POINTS DURING THE NEGOTIATION:

1) Don't be serious; always smile and always have a carefree attitude. You're almost flirting with her as you try and get her to be fair with you about prices.
2) You're willing to pay her and her establishment; but you know you are really doing HER the favor. Don't lose sight of this and don't be afraid to point it out if you need to. If you guys have some type of connection, it's not work to her, and being at the bar each night, unsure of the pay or the men that might come along, is WORK. This is a good deal for her regardless, and if she's not willing to take it there are many women out there who will. She, on the other hand doesn't get the opportunity to be paid for a week's vacation very often.

With bar girls, I take the same approach, but I lower the numbers across the board. I guess that the bar will charge her 2,000 baht for the week and she corrects me by saying around 3,000. I tell her I'm also willing to give her 5,000 baht for the week (roughly 700 a day), and she comes back with 7,000 or she just accepts my initial offer.

Don't pay up-front. You can pay her every day if you like; just avoid giving it to her all up-front. I'm not saying she'll run away with the money, although it has happened. But it's more of a psychological thing; if she has the money up-front she may not have the same desire to make things go as smooth as possible for you over the course of the next week.

Make sure you don't fall in love with the girl, and make sure you stick to your plan to end things once the week is over. If you don't you're not going to be the first or the last guy to make this mistake and you'll want to read further into Chapter 6 about what you're getting yourself into. Also during the week, make sure you guys get some space. She may be too shy to ask for it, but it's necessary for both of you. Give her 500 baht and tell her to go get her nails and hair done and to get a foot massage. It's a nice gesture and you'll both enjoy the time apart. I don't tip at the end in cash as many men do. If I really like the girl I bring her to the mall instead and I buy her some nice clothing. I don't want to be her typical customer, and just blindly handing her cash is as typical as it gets. As for what to do with this girl during the week, take a natural approach. You're paying for the girlfriend experience and you'll get what you pay for as long as you keep things calm and cool. Dinners, beach, a movie, bowling, drinks at a bar, a boat tour, a nice hike… these all make for nice ⅎ and your one-week girlfriend. Tell her to take you to a nice Buddhist temple, a ⁣ꜰ see a live band belt out some tunes from back home with a Thai or Pilipino ⁣you can also tell her to invite one of her friends to an early dinner with you. This ⁣ꜱ.y won't lead to a threesome, but she'll think it's very thoughtful and you'll appreciate having two ladies to spend some time with. You might be tempted not to use protection with this girl for the true girlfriend experience, and she may even go along with it, but you must use some self-control. Just because you are really getting to know her doesn't make it any less risky and it doesn't erase her past. If you insist, and I can't talk you out of it, you should at least take her to a clinic on the first day so the two of you can get "on-the-spot tests" done. She won't object, because she's been taught to frequently get tested and you're paying. Even if she passes, this is not necessarily accurate; she could still have HIV in its dormant stage if she contracted it within a month of the taking test. You also have other STD's to worry about besides HIV, such as chlamydia, and clinics may or may not have on-the-spot tests for those.

When the week comes to an end you might really like this girl and she might really like you. I continually suggest limiting how far you take this because the numbers don't lie, and most bar girls don't make good long-term companions, at least compared to non-prostitute Asian women. If you lack the will power to end it, read on in Chapter 6. But if you are ready to put the girl in your past, you need to finish paying her and you can share that last moment with her. I've told girls in this situation, "I'm not going to lie to you; I think you're amazing, you're perfect, but this is probably going to be the last time we see each other." It can be emotional, and not just for her. Nobody is made of stone. If this girl realizes how much better her life would be without the bar and she's fallen in love with you, it's going to be a tough spot for both of you. Give her something nice to go home with; possibly a present you picked up for her along the way, or you let her pick something out in the 2,000 baht range at a nice store. Say your goodbyes and let her become your "Go To Memory" when you're thinking about great times. That's the thing; when you end it with a girl like this after one week, you're really going out on a high note. You've most likely had a special time and so has she. If you try to keep it going, it will not continue and it'll be ruined. You'll no longer have the wonderful memory. Now you're both so sad and devastated that you go pick up another girl that night and she'll be with another customer that night as well. Actually, here is a good tip if you're on vacation and its coming to an end, as is the time you're spending with a great lady: leave at least a full night for yourself to see another lady before your trip is over so you go back with a level head and you get the proper perspective back. If you thought she was that great, put effort into meeting a traditional Thai, non-bar girl on your next trip and you'll find a soul mate for life.

Threesomes, Foursomes, Moresomes

If being with multiple women at one time has been a fantasy for you, this can be obtainable rather easily in Thailand. But, whether that experience becomes what you expected or a dud depends on the steps you take to set it up. There are bi-sexual women in Thailand, but the percentage of bi-sexual women in Western strip clubs is considerably higher than it is in Thai bars or GoGo's. All too often a man in Thailand pairs together two women he meets at a bar or a Gogo and expects things to go like they do in his imagination. It's easy enough to get two girls to come back with you since they both want to have a customer for the night, but once you're back with them it's going to be more like two one-on-ones than one threesome if you just wing it. And in talking to many dozens of people about this and experimenting a fair share of times myself, it seems that most men trying to orchestrate three-way magic usually wind up with two giggling, shy, and scared girls taking turns staying in the bathroom and being with you. And this happens even if they tell you differently at the bar or the Gogo you pick them up at.

Let's first differentiate between a wild threesome and the definition of one to most Thai women, or even to the establishments they work in. A wild threesome is one where all three of you are equally hot for each other and the man gets a little show before partaking in the fun, and there's a lot of sharing. When you get two girls in Thailand, even in a place that promotes you taking two ladies, they mostly look at it as two girls taking care of a man at the same time, but never taking care of each other. This can still be fun, but not quite what you had in mind.

If you want to increase the odds of having it go the way you really want it to, you want to avoid picking up two girls in the same place. There might be a rare exception of two girls who have prior lesbian experiences together who work at the same place, but mostly the girls who work together have no intentions of having a bi-sexual experience with each other. This is because they're most likely not bi-sexual, and even if they are or they're at least curious, they certainly don't want to experiment with a girl they'll have to see every day. So you want to start your night by talking to some women at Gogo's or bars. You may have more success at some of the low-end Gogo's where there is a higher percentage of true bi-sexual women. You're looking for a girl who openly admits to "liking girls." Luck will decide how many women you have to ask this question to before you find one who is clearly telling you the truth when she says, "Yes, I like girls." You can also see if a woman you already know from the bars is into women; if you do it could make things go even better. Either way you're not done with Step 1 until you have a girl who is definitely bi-sexual. Once you have met this woman, see if she's interested in having some fun with you and a girl to be found later. If she tells you that one of the girls she works with is perfect, resist this. She's more likely to be loyal to her friend in trying to get her a customer of sorts than she is to be honest with you about the hot steamy sex the three of you will have. If she specifically tells you she regularly gets down with a certain girl she's extremely attracted to, you should bar-fine her so the two of you can go look for a third teammate together. Negotiating her fee for the night should be the same as it would be if it was a one-on-one-only night, with the exception that you can mention that you'll give her a nice tip at the end of the night if all goes as planned.

So you leave the bar/Gogo where you picked up a hot bi-sexual who understands exactly what you're looking for and has incentive to make sure you get it. The best bet is to go to a low-end Gogo even if you just left one. Tell her you really need her to help you pick out a girl and to make sure the third girl is all aboard the wild crazy threesome train. True-blue bi-sexual women are pretty good at finding each other in this situation; she'll most likely be better at picking out the girl than you would be. As long as she doesn't pick a girl who you're not at all attracted to, you should let her lead the way. Even if the girl she has chosen isn't in love with women, as long as she has agreed to a REAL threesome this is going to work out well for you because the first girl you picked up is doing most of the work.

Make sure that the three of you aren't completely sober so that there is no anxiety in the air when you get back to your place. Alcohol has made many a threesome possible. Once you're at your hotel or condo there is no time for three separate showers, so the shower should be your first access to some craziness. After fourvery clean breasts leave the shower with you, go ahead and tell them that you want to watch them for a while. And from then on, the rest is up to you and you can do no wrong.

The whole process might sound easy, and that's because it is. Following the tips above you should be able to check "crazy wild threesome" off of your list of things you need to do at least once. Just make sure you have two condoms with you if you insist on having full sex, and not just oral, from both girls. Some girls will not want you to share a condom with them, and nobody can blame them for that.

Chapter 6: HAVING A THAI COMPANION

Don't be Stupid

There is a middle ground when it comes to an approach you should take in differentiating between Thai women who are suitable long-term companions and ones who are absolutely not suitable. I suppose the words cautious and guarded come to mind, as they would in any other countries, but **I would go as far as saying that there is a much higher percentage of women in Thailand who will make great girlfriends or wives than there is in the West.** The problem is that many men are only picking from a pool of ladies that worked or work in some form of prostitution, and by doing that they are drastically reducing the chances of having a good relationship. This has been discussed in the chapters above, and I am not saying that it is impossible to find a great wife who happens to work in a bar, I am just saying that it's unlikely, and that you open yourself up to many problems that are not prevalent amongst non-prostitute Thai women. Throughout the world, women look to men for financial security, but in Asia this trait is more openly discussed and accepted. Most men looking for a Thai wife will need to accept that one of the things she likes about him is the security he provides her. It's just important not to stay with a lady who prioritizes this one thing over everything else. The money/love priority line is important, but not always clear, as some women are better actresses than others. We can all accept that a woman wants to know that she won't starve and that her future children will have every basic opportunity to live a happy life. **Thus, a woman is entitled to have a minimum standard for financial attributes of a partner. The key is to pick a woman who doesn't care about financial things *beyond* that minimal standard.**

So let's discuss a silly example to further strengthen this all-important point. Let's say Bob is a wonderful man who can afford to support a family, but he's by no means wealthy and he can't provide luxuries. His future family will never worry about shelter, food, school, or the ability to be happy, but they won't be vacationing around the world and living in mansions. Then there's Joe, and Joe is not the nicest guy in the world. He's selfish and un-caring, and it's clear that he will never be faithful to his future wife. Joe also happens to be a very wealthy man who is capable of providing luxury for his wife. As crude an example as this is, if a woman picks Joe over Bob, she's not an ideal mate for a man. If she picks good ol' Bob over Joe, then her priorities are in check and her values aren't corrupted.

Any guesses on who a particular group of women would tend to choose from our example above, are just that, guesses. Even if we polled women, the poll would be compromised because they may like to think they'd pick Bob, but that doesn't mean they would when push comes to shove. It's pure conjecture, but I'll take a stab at guessing, and at the very least you should be able to take something out of my line of thinking. I would guess that 50 per cent of the women from your home country would pick Bob. I would guess that of all the Thai women who never worked in the pay-for-play industry, 75 per cent of them would pick Bob. And I would guess that out of only bar girls and Gogo girls in Thailand who worked a minimum of four months in the industry, 10 per cent would pick Bob. Ask some non-jaded expats in Thailand and they are likely to agree on my percentages. Oh, and if a third man, Jim, was the best looking and nicest guy in the world but completely broke, I actually think 25 per cent of women back home would go with Jim, and I don't think there are any Thai women that would. Again, I think that's fine because they're entitled to have a minimum standard and expectation of financial security for the well-being of their future children.

You need to be honest with yourself and you need to be smart. Bar girls tell a lot of guys they love them. If a bar girl quickly tells you she loves you, there just isn't much of a chance that it's actually true. Most people will make sacrifices for love. A bar girl may like you a lot, but would she be willing to make any sacrifices for your well-being? Test her; ask her if she can pay for everything for a few weeks while you get your finances together. She's going to fail that test. Or tell her you just can't afford to go out with her anymore so you'll both have to stay in or find free activities to enjoy from now on, and shopping is totally off the table. You think she'll stick around a while after telling her that?

The sad thing is that Thai prostitutes don't really respect most Western men, and just see them as suckers who can foolishly spend their money on a lady. There's actually a saying here that can be translated to mean, "Farang who come and spend money here on vacation are good; Farang that know too much about Thailand are bad." My further translation of this is, "If a man is wise to things there is no chance you can con him; if he's some dumb schmuck looking for love you can milk him."

Yes there are some examples of women who worked in bars but turned into great wives, and there are also examples of non-prostitute Thai women who have turned into terrible wives. It's just a lot less likely to be the other way around.

If I wrote about each example of a story I'd heard or witnessed of a man being in a very bad situation thanks mostly to believing a bar girl loved him, this book would become more like an encyclopedia. It happens all of the time. The phrase, "A fool and his money are soon parted," rings a bell. If a fool comes here, inevitably there will be a pack of Thai people in a village soon living the good life off his money and laughing at him while they do it. So rather than me just drilling it into your head that you need to stay guarded for another 100 pages, and rather than writing 700 pages of real life stories that will scare you straight, I will just provide a generic outline for the basis of what tends to happen; then I'll break down how to handle most situations regarding a Thai mate, one-by-one, so that you are always in the driver's seat.

How it starts

So most of them start like this:

A Man comes to Thailand on vacation. The man is single or divorced and hasn't been laid in a while, and he doubts he can find love in his country ever again. He meets a pretty bar girl and begins a relationship with her. After a week or two, he and the lady both profess their love for each other and the man arranges to keep some sort of long-distance relationship going when his vacation ends. The woman soon says that she wants to marry him and she is lost without him and doesn't want to go back to the bar or be with another man ever again. The man agrees to pay her enough money to live without having to go to the bar while she "looks for some type of job." Whether she finds a job or not, the job wouldn't even come close to paying all of her monthly expenditures (according to her), so the man continues to send money while he prepares his next vacation to Thailand. By this point he might have bought her a laptop and might be paying for an internet connection so they can communicate by video chat for free. The man finally arrives back in Thailand where he and the woman have the time of their lives on his buck for a few weeks. The woman is nearly flawless throughout the entire stint. His vacation ends and he is madly in love with the girl and the feeling seems to be mutual.

The man goes back home, and about the only thing he can think about is his Thai love. By now there might have been a few people who have warned him that he needs to be careful. He tunes most of this out, but his friends manage to convince him to at least not get married or move to Thailand right away. So he continues to pay the woman each month and keeps a long distance relationship going with her as he saves up when he's home so that he can visit her in Thailand as often as he can. He spends as little as is possible, so really ever dollar he makes is either going towards his bare survival needs, her cost of living, or his vacations to Thailand where he splurges on her. Each time he comes home becomes more depressed than the last, and by now he has usually started dipping into his savings.

And here is where the story diverges into two possible places:

Possibility 1

After this process goes on for over a year, possibly even for multiple years, something happens which causes it to end. He may pick up on something when he's over there; maybe his girlfriend has been ignoring many incoming phone calls, or maybe he catches her speaking English to someone on the phone. Perhaps he looks at her email account on the laptop he bought her and finds dozens of emails that break his heart into pieces. Or maybe the girl asks for a large sum of money and the man becomes suspicious. He interrogates her and the woman is not able to properly answer the questions, so the man knows she's lying. The man has already spent a great deal of his money on the girl before realizing that she has never been honest with him, and he manages to get out of the situation damaged, but not finished. He had some good times with the girl regardless of her intentions, and he still has a job at home and a chance at some sort of life. The end of the relationship will cause stress and possibly depression, but it's nothing the man can't eventually overcome. Does the man ever completely figure out that the woman had two other men in her pocket from overseas the whole time? Or that the woman continued to freelance and go with five to ten customers a week? Or that she's had a Thai boyfriend or even a husband this whole time that he's been supportingher? He may figure all of this out, but it may be better if he didn't.

Possibility 2

The man can no longer deal with the thought of being without the woman and is now dead set on either moving to Thailand or moving his girlfriend to his country. After some online investigating he sees that moving her to his country isn't going to work long-term unless he marries her and then goes through a very long, difficult and expensive process. He and the woman question whether she'd be happy in a new country. He realizes that the happiest and best times of his life have been IN THAILAND WITH HIS GIRLFRIEND, so he decides to quit his job, pack his things, and move to Thailand to be with his girlfriend. After liquidating many of his possessions (possibly including his house), the man has money in his savings and he knows he can get by for a decade or longer on them since Thailand is so cheap. He also plans on getting a job and is sure that his future wife will eventually bring in some sort of income.

And this actually can go into two different places as well:

Possibility 2a

Upon arriving in Thailand, he sets out to find the perfect place for himself and his future wife to live in. She soon teaches him that it's unsafe for him to buy a property because he can only own 49 per cent as a foreigner, but luckily the wife is 100 per cent Thai, so he buys a house under her name. As they look into a wedding, it turns out that the woman's family is in crisis: her aunt and favorite person in the world is very sick and will die unless she has expensive surgery. Also, her brother has been accepted to one of the best universities in the country, which means he'll be able to support their parents very well one day, but alas he can't even go because they don't have enough money for tuition. Basically, the woman keeps going until either there is nothing left or until the man says "NO", or the man wakes up and realizes what's going on. In this situation, the woman never intended to marry him. Actually she preferred him to stay in his country sending the reliable monthly stipend, but the man had to mess up that revenue stream by actually coming to Thailand. So she, with the help of her Thai boyfriend or one of her family members, comes up with ways to get as much as she can out of the guy before he realizes they aren't getting married or becomes broke. The man now goes back to his home country with no job, a lack of respect from anyone who knows what happened, and a gigantic hit to his net worth if not a total annihilation of it.

Possibility 2b

The man arrives in Thailand and immediately takes the steps necessary to marry his girlfriend. He meets her family and things are generally going well. He begins teaching, the pay isn't great and it isn't easy, but it provides some much needed income and it's somewhat rewarding. Before the wedding, the wife and/or her family probe into his financial situation, and since he's about to be married to the woman, he tells the truth about his savings. The family then comes up with a proper dowry for the man to pay at their wedding to their family. The man doesn't know it but he's actually paying five times more dowry for his uneducated former prostitute than some men are paying for a very educated virgin. He asks about this and is quickly told that it's a Thai custom and he must do it as a sign of his love and shouldn't ask or complain about it. The man pays for the entire wedding and there seems to be a whole village of people enjoying themselves on his dollar. Now is when the fun starts; immediately the man is cornered and pressured to pay his wife's family every month, and this is also a "Thai custom". The wife isn't acting anything like she did prior to the wedding. She seems lazy, relatively unloving, and she is coming right out and asking for him to buy her things. She doesn't work and is obviously not being honest about her numerous "job interviews". Then there is usually some type of "family catastrophe" and some type of "brilliant can't-miss business opportunity," all requiring significant amounts of money. After a year or two goes by, the man can no longer deal with the woman and her family. He knows they are abusing him and he finally begins to stand up for himself, if not for his pride then for his dwindling savings. His fight to make things right is met with, "Fine if you don't like it, then we should divorce." The woman takes the business and the home and that is that. If he had a child with her during this time, it adds to the complexity of the exit strategy. He either abandons the child completely so that he never feels good about himself ever again, or he does the right thing and continues to support the child. The Mother uses it as a bargaining chip to continue to skim funds from him for twenty years while working as a prostitute, which doesn't make his child feel all that special.

Naturally, the girls who turn to prostitution don't usually have the best family situations , so it's not only that she has a good chance to be unscrupulous, but her family also has a significantly better chance of turning out to be a thorn in your side as well. The family was never interested in her well-being and had no problem accepting money from her each month as their daughter was defiled by foreign men. So if this is the case, it stands to reason that they will never respect you as a caretaker to their daughter, and may even resent you for taking away her contributing income. They will do whatever it takes to get every baht they can out of you until you're finished, and they'll get a few laughs at your expense when it's all over. There have been plenty of relationships where the former bar girl did turn the corner and become a good wife, but things still ended disastrously, thanks to her family.

And for every bar girl and bar girl's family like this, there are ten non-bar girls who have a good family and who you will be proud to call family. Knowing all of this you should be able to draw the logical conclusion that if you are in search of a wife, you want to begin that search outside of the bars. There will be people who just don't get it and do it anyway, and there will be people who "didn't mean to fall in love; it just happened." There may even be a few people reading this who are already stuck in a bad situation. So, here is my breakdown of what to do if you are faced with a few possible scenarios.

Relationship with a bar girl/Gogo dancer 1

You want to see how it goes with a bar girl/Gogo dancer for a while and you're here for an extended period of time

If you have had the time of your life with a girl you just met, who am I to tell you not to continue on that high note? I would go with a one-week limit in regard to any bar girl, but I suppose double that wouldn't be so bad in a rare exception. You don't want to make things hard on yourself though, and the more time you spend with the girl the harder it might be to end things. It shouldn't be that way as you are paying for her time, but it *is* that way, especially if she has given up short-term goals, such as charging you daily, for more long-term goals, such as getting something monthly from you. It could really feel like you have a real girlfriend, and I suppose there are elements there that would give those feelings some validity. But by the time one month rolls around, the nice shiny-new-car feeling will certainly have lost its luster and you'll be looking more clearly at a woman who primarily wants you for your money, and who has been with hundreds of men for the same reason. Or, you'll be in love with the girl and totally blind to anything negative about her, but let's hope that's not the case.

If you want to continue to see a girl here for a while, you'll first have to decide if you're willing for her to continue working in her job satisfying foreign clientele from time to time, or if you want to completely shut that part of her life down while you see her. Obviously the cost of doing the latter will be up there. If we're talking about anything up to two weeks, you can refer to **Chapter 5,** in the section entitled **The End-game No. 3: Thank you, stay for a while.** If we're talking about more than that, you'll need to set up some sort of plan and fee structure. If you're ok with her getting other clients then you can agree on a fair rate for her to see you however often per week or per month you'd like to, including bar fines. Some men that already have a full-time girlfriend choose to do this with their "Go-To Bar girl" on the side. This makes things more affordable and more discreet than going with new women all of the time, but once in a while the woman won't pick up the phone for you because she'll already be with a customer. You should always call her before she starts work to make arrangements. If you plan on meeting her once her shift is done to avoid the bar fines, this doesn't mean she wasn't with a short-term customer that night, but it also doesn't mean that you weren't with your full-time girlfriend that night either, so all is fair.

If you want to keep things going just to see how they go past a couple of weeks, and you don't want to share the bar girl with any other customers, you'll need to figure something else out. It will never work out if she works in the bar each night getting lady drinks, with you shelling out the occasional bar fine so her Mamasan is happy. Many have tried this and it always winds up in failure, because she is constantly propositioned by potential customers and this is just unhealthy for your relationship. You might need to pay a "buy-out" to her bar so that she can get a job there again if it doesn't work out with the two of you. And by doing this they'll release whatever funds they owe her. The woman sends her family money each month, and now that's your job. She also "saves" some money each month, so now that's your job too. Yes, you'll literally be putting money into her savings. And she'll make it like this isn't "GETTING PAID" to be with you because this is just money that she relies on for retirement, and that she would lose if you take her away from her "job." On top of this you'll continue to pay for her rent and she'll likely charge you more than it really is. You'll also be paying for every little thing when the two of you are together, and she'll expect to live pretty well when she's with you. You can keep that pace going for a total of up to three months if you're crazy enough. At that point it either has to end or it has to evolve into something even more long-term. If you're not in love with the girl then you're in good shape and you can just end it after having spent way too much money, but nothing that'll negatively impact your life. If you are in love with her, you have a whole new set of problems which I'll discuss after the next section.

Just remember that if you are in some type of longer-term phase with a bar girl (past the two-week mark but less than the three-month mark), you have to be committed to saying no to any over-the-top requests, such as family medical emergencies, new motorbike, school tuitions (she's not going back to school and even if she did its dirt-cheap here), etc. And as a matter of fact, once one of these requests is made you should take your cue to immediately end things, rather than just saying "No." If your head is on straight you'll be looking for any reason to end things rather than being impossibly stupid and looking for any reasons to keep things going. There are literally hundreds of thousands of Thai women who you can have a fun time with and not break the bank (bar girls and non-bar girls alike), so why would you spend excessive cash just to keep it going with a girl you know you're not going to end up with? Some guys fall into patterns and they like a little familiarity; they don't want to be alone and they like having a prolonged girlfriend experience. But anything over two weeks is too much, and anything past three months is absurd. Again, if you're not truly in love with the girl you have to end it, and you'll get over your sadness by going out with a new girl the next day as she goes home with a new customer. If you are in love, as I mentioned, I'm getting to that.

Relationship with a bar girl/Gogo dancer 2

You want to keep things going with a Thai bar girl but you can only come once or twice a year.

You have read this book and you can accept that there is no way to keep her loyal and faithful to you once you leave, but that doesn't stop you from wanting to keep in touch with her, and it also doesn't stop you from wanting to be with her when you are there. You won't let anything get out of control, but you want the girlfriend experience to continue, and you would like to have someone to talk to once in a while when you're home, as well as someone to see you when you vacation in Thailand. This isn't highly recommended, but it can easily be worse, so I'll give you a couple of things to look out for. She's not just going to keep a relationship going with you out of the goodness of her heart, past an email or phone call or two. But my rule in this book is to never send money unless you're with her, and you should never break this rule. So if you're dead set on making it work this way, you will need to give her a considerable tip when you part ways in Thailand, and let her know that there'll be another one just like it the next time you come. I suppose this can be something like 20,000 to 30,000 baht. And all you get for that money is someone to talk to once in a while on the phone or video chat, and the high probability of there being someone you like available for you to spend your next vacation with. She will still see customers and she probably has someone sending her cash each month (sponsor); she probably has a Thai boyfriend, to boot. But you don't care and it's worth the 25,000 baht for you to have a kind of flim-flam long-distance relationship. I have seen this before, and coincidentally the couple of guys I know that did this happened to have wives back home, and they insisted that they just needed someone they liked to be there once in a while to talk to so they could keep their sanity. I guess the girl functions as a not-too-expensive quasi-mistress . One of the guys said that he and the girl would have crazy video chats together sometimes, and those were more than worth the big tips in themselves. Whatever the case, I agree that this isn't such a bad option as it is mostly controlled and there is a limited downside.

You are in love with a bar girl, now what?

The short answer is to cut your losses and run. I have even suggested that you bar-fine another girl for a day, or even longer, once the relationship ends with a girl you had strong feelings for. But if there is just no stopping you from continuing your relationship with her, then we should at least take steps to make the experience as painless as possible.

First of all, if you are in your country and you have ignored my advice and are paying your bar girl money thinking she is absolutely being loyal and faithful to you, then please at least invest some money in a service that will investigate whether this is actually true. There are links for such services in Chapter 17. While you're looking at those, go and read some case studies. Not only do most bar girls end up being caught lying about everything, but sometimes the guys are so crazy that they don't even believe it when the evidence is in their face, and they believe every excuse the girls gives them when confronted. Such a man is not destined to hold on to his cash or his mental health. Sometimes the girl isn't actively getting customers because you and her other bone-headed sponsors are giving her so much money that she gets to live the good life. If she is the one in a hundred (that's being nice) and the investigation finds the bar girl is loyal, faithful, and doesn't have other sponsors, then you only need to worry about her family and friends (a group that had no problem with her being a hooker) eventually wearing her down and changing her tune with you. What will happen in the end? What will you get out of it? Are you going to marry her, quit your job, and move to Thailand while lying to everyone you know about her former occupation? Will you go through a nearly impossible process to marry her and bring her to your country where she won't fit in or meet new friends and resent you for making her unhappy? There's absolutely no benefit from paying the girl any money while you aren't in Thailand, and the only thing that would be worse, would be to change your whole life around a girl destined to destroy you. At least if you live in Thailand before you meet her you have plenty of time to see how things go. But if you're overseas, Thai girls often take advantage of the distance and use it to manipulate you.

Who am I forgetting to represent? How about the guy out there who meets a bar girl, goes back home while he fully supports her and she's loyal to him? In this situation the man visits as often as possible, and when things make sense he eventually goes to live happily ever after with her, or she comes to his country and they live happily ever after. They never get pressure from her family for money and she never gets out of line in what she asks for either. She doesn't ever complain to him about how her many bar lady friends' parents get 30,000 a month from their husbands, and she never threatens to leave with the children if she doesn't get what she wants financially. I suppose this has happened before and it may happen again, but anything can happen. I can put everything I am worth on a number in roulette and there is a 1-in-38 chance (thanks 0 + 00) that I will multiply my assets by 36 times. If 38 people were crazy enough to take this risk, 1 of them would be a very happy guy, and 37 of them would have ruined their lives. If I'm writing to an audience that is considering doing the same roulette gamble, it would make a lot more sense for me to talk about what happens 37 times out of 38, rather than to talk about how happy the 1 guy out of 38 is. This example illustrates my feelings on the matter, but it may not even be extreme enough because the one lucky guy in the example never had a chance to WIN THAT BIG in life without that substantial risk. But if you're the 1 in 38 who puts everything on the line for a bar girl with it eventually paying off in the long run, it still doesn't mean that you couldn't have found the very same thing or better with another non-bar girl without risking anything. The odds just don't stack up well.

Now, the exception is if the girl wasn't in the industry long and you have confirmed this perhaps with an investigation. You really should investigate any girl you want to make a push to be with for a long time if she was in the bar industry for any length of time. And if you live in Thailand or you have the flexibility in your schedule and your bank account to visit Thailand many times each year, then it can be a bit different as well. If you give it ample time, a year or more, before you even think about getting married, and the two of you have lived together for the most part over the duration, you should get a decent picture of how things will work. Con-artists and their families might be willing to be patient if there is a big score looming, but their patience will have run out short of a year and you'll get hit up for something that doesn't sound right, which will confirm all suspicions. Again, if after fifteen or twenty months of living with a former bar girl the two of you are just as happy as can be, her background investigation is clean, and her family does not require that she and you support them, then you might very well have a genuine relationship with this woman where marriage can be considered. I'm not opposed to this at all; I just find it to be rare, especially since most foreigners are not living in Thailand when they meet the bar girl they fall in love with, which is off the table in my book. **Basically I am only OK with you marrying a bar girl if you have lived with her for a long time and have confirmed that her friends, family, and her background are all non-issues.** Anything short of that isn't a good idea.

To give it any shot of working out you'll need to be tough with her on issues that other saps and suckers wouldn't. She needs to know up-front that if you are ever asked for any type of large sum of money for her family, you will not pay it, even if it means that Aunt Noy dies as a result. You should even make sure her family is aware of this. She needs to also know that you are well aware of how things work in Thailand, and that if she's out to get a sucker she's currently spinning her wheels going the opposite direction. Tell her that although she may think lying to you is no problem, if you catch her doing it often you'll end things without warning. Set limits with her on spending, and limits must never be broken. If she asks to break a limit, you say "NO", and you see how she responds. If she ever complains to you about how her other bar friends are being treated and how she wants the same from you, you tell her that if she ever brings this up again you will be gone as quick as she can make Pad Thai. That is essential and she needs to believe it! You need to establish almost immediately that you are not going to be bullied in any way. If she doesn't like it she can go back to selling herself to a dozen guys per week on her way to a horrible life. If you're not using a condom she may try and get pregnant to trap you into marriage, which is not uncommon in any country. Tell her that if you catch her not taking her birth control pill that you'll have to end things.

Also if marriage is in the works, she and her family need to know that you'll give what you feel is appropriate as a dowry, and that if they complain about it or ask for more, then you might have to think about giving nothing. A girl with no university degree who worked at a bar shouldn't get more than 100,000 baht, 200,000 at the most, and that's excessive. Because of her former profession they should get 0, but I think it's worth the 100,000 baht dowry to avoid a blow up confrontation over. If the family tells you they want you to give more, just in show (to impress people), and that they'll return it immediately after the wedding, this is fine. Maybe you give them 300,000 baht and they will give you 200,000 baht back after the wedding. If they go against their word and don't give

you the money back, then you remind them that they owe you that money and that they will never see a single baht from you or their daughter ever again until it is paid back. Perhaps in that case you'd be lucky if they don't give it to you as you're off the hook from then on.

If you take this approach you will be met with the same old spiel from her friends or family about how in Thailand its different and you must show your love by giving lots of money and being "less serious". And that your future wife is "losing face" because of your actions. You just need to get the following message across:

1) You will be an ideal husband. You will never yell, hit or abuse your wife. You will always provide for her and you will do whatever it takes to make her happy and to keep her safe. You will be an amazing father to her future children and they will never have to worry about them or their daughter.
2) You are adapting to the "Thai culture" by paying some sort of dowry despite the fact that it's clearly not necessary to do so as she was a prostitute and is not educated. You are also paying for the wedding despite the fact that it's against YOUR CULTURE to do so.
3) They should be happy that their daughter/friend is in good hands with a man who doesn't easily get suckered into things. You are cautious and careful and this is great for their daughter in the long term.

Now, if your girlfriend or wife has a bad pack of friends and family members, they're not really going to care about any of that, but at least you put it out there. Now when they say they don't care, you can say , "That's fine because I don't care that you don't care." Most of the time they take all of the control away from the farang and it works, but you are the one guy who realizes the very obvious: you are actually the one in complete control. If they don't like it they get nothing. Easy. If they leave you alone then they keep their dowry and you may permit your wife to send them a very small amount each month without ever breaking your limit. If you get any pressure to send more or to send a lump-sum payment then you stop your monthly stipend for one month and tell them that each time they ask for more ,there will be another month in which they get nothing. This means you'll always have control, and as much as they try to convince you of how bad a man you are because you're so "serious and cheap", the truth is that they will actually have respect for you in time, especially if they see that your wife is happy and very well-cared for. It's all about establishing the whole "feel" of this from the very beginning, and not relenting. If you slip its likely you'll have to do some damage-control to get things back on track; it makes a lot more sense to never get off the path.

You want to find your soul-mate or bride

If you skipped right to this section shortly after starting the book, then you're looking for love and nobody can blame you for that. With the tips throughout the book and in this section, you can find a wonderful woman here. And from reading even just a little of this book, you know that starting in the bars and in the Gogos is not your best bet. Neither is the internet for the most part. There may be some decent match-maker websites out there, but the unscrupulous ones that put fake pretty women into their database outnumber the solid ones. You open yourself up to scams and fees on the internet as well, and I think there are much better ways. To find an ideal mate you should first make a few concessions.

The best brides in Thailand will probably...

1) Not speak much English
2) Not do a lot of fun activities
3) Not be outgoing with you in the beginning
4) Not understand your sense of humor
5) Not shave the way women do at the bars
6) Not dress trendy
7) Not put out for a while
8) Never be overly experimental in bed

You shouldn't find that list to be too difficult to get past, looking at the corresponding list below.

The best brides in Thailand will probably...

1) Learn English quickly and with a passion
2) Appreciate learning and finding new hobbies and activities with a little push into them
3) Be as loving with you as can be once she has warmed up to you
4) Eventually adapt to your sense of humor, and will find you to be quite humorous
5) Won't take offense to your recommended shaving patterns
6) Will enjoy getting some new clothing from a cheap market and won't ask for anything.
7) Remind you that the best things are worth waiting for
8) Never yell at you the day after a daring sexual act, because they won't happen in the first place.

Additionally, the best brides in Thailand...

1) Will take good care of themselves and will stay slim
2) Tend to be very pleasant
3) Are wizards when it comes to any type of housework
4) Are hard-working and capable when they need to be
5) Are always 100% dedicated to their family
6) Treat their husbands with respect
7) Have a healthy sexual appetite
8) Don't ask and complain about ridiculous things like, "Why don't you buy me a Mercedes?"
9) Avoid divorce like the plague
10) Genuinely show appreciation

So I guess that just leaves the question, "Where do I find one like that?" The anywhere **BUT** bars, Gogo's and massage parlors. I will give you a good pla ~~law~~ everything is on the table. If a cute girl is working at a 7-11, it means she is worki money when she could be doing very little work for big money at a bar, which is a h_ _ ,ius. It also means that she doesn't have any negative pressure coming from her family and friends to do something unethical. And lastly, it would mean that she'd appreciate a lot more things than women in the West or in the bars. I'm not telling you to recruit out of a 7-11, the point I'm making is that Thai women tend to be fantastic long-term mates outside of the pay-for-play industry, and that you can meet them almost anywhere. They'll be shy and some of them may have a boyfriend or a husband. But as long as you're not shy and you find a way to interact with them, you'll quickly figure out if they're single and if they're willing to go to dinner with you. Many girls here who have legitimate jobs are not used to being asked out by a farang or getting treated to a beautiful dinner, so your odds aren't bad.

If you don't have a lot of time to date and meet girls the natural way, you might be inclined to take a few short cuts to meet your future bride. Some Thai experts may say the following plan is silly, but I have seen it work at a success rate that has made me a true believer. In fact I believe the naysayers might just be jealous that they didn't do it themselves. We already know that you can go to any city and any town and meet great women who have never been a prostitute, in a similar way to meeting women in the West, by talking to them and asking them out on a date. Your success rate of doing that will be te times higher than in your home town, but this may still be too much work for some, especially those with limited time. For those folks, here is what I would do. Go to Isan. Set up shop there for a few weeks. I'm not going to specify places as that is not necessary, you just need to be near what seems to be some sort of civilization with some sort of hotels and the occasional McDonalds. If they have a movie theatre very nearby then you're in the right place. If there isn't a movie theatre or a bowling alley within dozens of miles, then you are too far into the depths of Isan.

Once you're in Isan you're going to want to identify someone who can help you for you for a reasonable amount of money. The best bet is a popular older woman in her early 60s. These women know everyone, but their only downside might be limited English so you'll also need to find someone who can do a bit of translating for you. Isan is very poor, and a few hundred baht here and there goes a long way. You want to make it clear to the woman, and everyone else for that matter, that you love Thailand and you are looking for a beautiful Thai bride. Offer her 1,000 baht a day to start spreading the word and introducing you to pretty women who never worked in a bar and were never married. I would talk to those who have college under their belt just the same as I would those who don't, as long as they are employed. Make sure the woman knows you will provide her with a very nice bonus if she finds you one that has great potential. I am sure that within a couple of days the word will spread like wild fire and you'll have more interested girls than you'll know what to do with. There are match-maker services that do exactly the same thing only they charge a hell of a lot more and you don't have any control. Don't underestimate a popular older woman's reach in the villages. Phone calls will be made and they'll find you a lady. You just need to make sure she gets fairly paid for her time, but doesn't take advantage of you in the process.

Once you meet a fantastic lady it would be best if you can spend some time in Thailand with the lady you click with before making a decision on whether or not you would like to marry her. They'll marry you almost on the spot if that's what you're looking for, but it's important that you make sure you have a game plan. Are you going to live in Thailand? If so, then it's fairly straight forward, and a in Thailand will help you through a fairly easy process of getting a visa. If you intend to take back to your country it will be much more difficult in terms of visas and paperwork, and I'll expand on that in the next section. It will be difficult to keep a long-distance relationship going with a woman who doesn't speak English and doesn't know what your level of commitment is. But if you have to go home for at least a few months and you're not ready to get married, get engaged. No harm no foul there. You can tell her that planning the wedding and the visas and things will take a while and in the mean time you should both get to know each other better, hopefully with some sort of video chat, such as Skype.

Throughout the book I have made it clear, in regards to bar girls, that you never give money unless you are with her. It's slightly different if you're with a regular Thai lady. You can be much more trusting, but you should never be completely trusting of any woman until you know her inside and out. So you might want to make sure she has a computer with video chat available to her, or at least give her money to go to internet cafes to chat with you. I just really don't like the idea of getting into a monthly "allowance" figure, so if you're going to give money as a sign of commitment, you're better off giving a lump sum to her in person just before leaving. Tell her the money is for her to have as a "just-in-case fund". If you're thinking strongly about marrying the girl, get the background check and investigation done (links provided in Chapter 17). Don't feel guilty about doing this. If you had the time to date her for a year and live with her for another year with no pressure of marriage then you wouldn't get an investigation done, but in this case you need to take some precaution to account for what you cannot possibly find out on your own under the circumstances.

You also need to feel around for the family situation. Make sure their head is in a good place and they don't look at you as if they just hit the lottery. You'll want to be strong about your convictions; you're not going to just hand over money because they demand it. Some women help support their families out of custom and necessity. She may expect you to make that contribution on her behalf each month. As long as it's less than 15,000 baht per month (hopefully it's more like 8,000 to 10,000) then you can agree to this if you feel comfortable in doing so. You should know that many families don't need the help and don't want the help, and that's the kind of family I would personally want to marry into, but sometimes you don't get that option with a woman you love, and this is understandable. If you are agreeing to a monthly sum for her family they need to know up-front that if they ever ask for more you will probably stop the payments all together. You'll come off as stern and they'll complain that you're "too serious", but you'll have done yourself a huge favor down the road by letting them know that you're not the kind of farang sucker they've heard about. You'll also need to pay a dowry since she wasn't a bar girl, and especially if she was never married, has no children, and has a college degree. I talked about the dowry as it relates to bar girls where you should pay as little as possible just to squash the situation. Regarding non-bar girls, you may have to pay up. It depends on her family though, and they may not want it. They may give you it back the day after the wedding, or at least give you a chunk back. But, they may also expect it and want to keep it especially since you are not Thai. My rule is not to go higher than 300,000. The exception would be if the girl is gorgeous, college-educated, a virgin, and is already making a nice salary in Thailand; for a girl like this you might have to pay 500,000. But if she's not completely perfect in every way like that, 300,000 is the limit, and you should not start with that if there is a negotiation process. Start lower, knowing you may end up there. Some expats will incorrectly tell you that such limits are disrespectful and will embarrass your wife and her family and that you must pay whatever they want. That's totally insane; you can easily find a great girl whose parents don't want anything from you, and they'll take what you give them in the end. I actually think having a little feud over the dowry is good because you get the opportunity to establish your rules about giving money from the get-go. Again, you give what you can and what you're willing to, and do not get taken advantage of. Go back and read the section of this chapter called **"You are in love with a bar girl, now what?"** which explains how to handle the dowry with a bar girl's family. The only difference with a non-bar girl is that you're giving the family more of a benefit of the doubt about their respect for you, so you're willing to give more money. But you should be equally tough about your limits in both cases. And if the woman complains about you not giving her family as much as some other farang do, then you need to make it clear that if she complains again about this and compares you to other farang (presumably suckers who will wind up broke and in a depression after a few years) that you'll stop ALL of the money to her family. You'll be a great husband to this woman, but you're not going to let her family take advantage of you, and you must always insist that she never compares what they or she GETS to what other farang give.

If you are going to marry a Thai woman you should invest in a prenuptial agreement that is written in both Thai and English. If it's not in Thai, she can get out of the contract because she can say she didn't know what she was signing. In this case I would consult with a lawyer who specializes in Thailand and in your home country to be on the safe side. Marriage is serious business and you can't let love make you forget it. You'll probably live happily ever after if you meet a great Thai woman, but you still need to be smart and cautious.

*** I only endorse two businesses in Thailand officially, and I won't even list them in the book since this isn't ad space.

1) If you need a very affordable and old school match-maker in Isan to find you a beautiful non-bar girl as a long term spouse or wife, please let me know and I'll get you the details.

2) If you're under 50 and you think you're going to run into visa issues, I know a place that has the perfect solution.

So if you want to talk further about either of these two things, make sure you email me at: info@thaigirlspattayagirls.com

Bringing your Thai wife back to your home country

The process to make this possible depends on your country's laws, and typically the U.S. is known for its process being the most lengthy and difficult, but it's an undertaking in just about any country. Some countries have some minimum requirements in terms of your financial situation. They want to be assured that your future wife is not going to become a burden to the system, so you must show proof of income, some assets, and perhaps no recent bankruptcies. Criminal background issues may also come into play depending on the location. It unfortunately isn't as simple as getting married and moving. First you will undoubtedly face a mountain of fees and paperwork to get her over on some type of temporary visa, where you can then begin the steps to make her a permanent citizen, which will not happen overnight. It's important to understand that marrying a woman from any other country will always be a large task, so this isn't a knock on marrying a Thai woman, it's a problem faced with any type of international marriage. Money, diligence, patience, and a good lawyer will always get the job done in the end. You can start by going to your country's embassy site to see if the process will even be possible for you. If so, then your next step is to seek a good immigration attorney who specializes in fiancé/marriage visas.

Relating specifically to Thai women, I only have two warnings: First, if you intend to spend half of the year in Thailand and half of the year in your home country (as many people wish to do), you will run into many visa issues from the beginning, and it may take a long time before you can do this consistently in full confidence without being overwhelmed by paperwork and fees. So if you intend to move your Thai wife to your country, it is highly recommended that you both go into it with an understanding that you will be living in your home country for the foreseeable future, and that travel back to Thailand won't happen often at first, and if it does it will be for vacation, and not for lengthy periods of time.

Second, there seems to be a notion that Thai women become unhappy in Western countries such as the U.S. and Britain, at least when comparing them to women who are more eager to leave their countries in South and Central America, as well as some of Eastern Europe. Thai women just aren't desperate to leave. They're safe and warm in Thailand and they have their family and friends there. They might be more intimidated by the new country than excited by it. Women in Mexico fear for their lives, and women in Romania deal with terrible winters and rampant poverty. These are just two examples of many where a lady would do anything to get American citizenship. We all know that Thailand is a wonderful place, so the ladies might quickly find more negatives than positives in their new home. This isn't to say that it's not possible for her to be happy, of course it is. But if she's unhappy, the burden will usually come down on you. And in any event you'll need to put a lot of effort into making her adjustment as manageable as possible. Issues of friends, work, driving and language are going to come into play, and you'll have to deal with them because she won't be well equipped to do so on her own. If you can find another Thai woman in your country, perhaps one that also lives with a "farang" husband, this will help. Having one good friend would really make things substantially better for her adjustment.

How to keep seeing bar girls/go go girls, while you have a Thai girlfriend or wife.

Believe it or not it's the former bar girls who would give you the most trouble in terms of seeing other women. Perhaps this is because they know the tricks of the trade or because their trust in men has taken a hit forever. Whatever the case, bar girls may always be slightly suspicious of your behavior and you may find it difficult to get the space you need to "operate." The more traditional Thai girl who has never worked in a bar will be far easier to keep happy as you do what you have to do behind her back. It is generally more accepted by Thai wives for their husbands to cheat with a mistress or a prostitute than it would be by Western women. This doesn't mean she'll be totally OK with it, but it means there is a good chance that she won't act like a detective every day.

There are a few basic things that you can do to make sure you are never caught red-handed. Here is a list:

1) Don't assume your wife can't read English. She may not be able to, but she can get someone else to translate for her if she finds something suspicious.

2) Never give your wife your email password. If she asks for it you tell her that's an intrusion as many of your family members and old friends talk about private issues with you and you're not about to betray their trust.

3) Do not leave your email account open, always make sure you log out. And just in case, if you have emails you want to keep that you don't want her to see, bury them inside a secret folder hidden inside a boring-sounding folder. Do the same for files on your computer and don't forget that many guys have been caught by the "recent items" results from the Windows Start menu.

4) Have a password on your phone; and you should delete all texts and emails that you get on there that you don't want her to see.

5) Never bring a girl back to your own apartment or house; Thai girls shed hair with the best of them and trust me when I say that they can tell the difference between strands of their hair vs. someone else's. I had a couple of girls wear hair nets after I got caught the first time this way, but I eventually realized how much better a hotel would be anyway. Between perfume smell and the possibility of a girl leaving something behind such as a hair clip, it's just too much to worry about the morning after. This is if you don't live with a girl or she's out of town. Get yourself a hotel room; if budget is a concern there are always cheap rooms available all over Thailand. If you have a long-term girlfriend, you certainly don't need to impress a bar girl with a nice room.

6) Don't mess around with anyone who is even remotely connected to your Thai girlfriend. Jealousy will cause the word to get around.

7) If you know you're the type who consistently needs a fix, you need to establish some sort of pre-packaged excuse for why you may need to spend nights out from the beginning of your relationship. The easiest is to say that you do a little business in Bangkok and in China that involves sending cheap goods to your country whenever your customers put in orders. So if you want one night out, you can say you're headed to Bangkok and you'll be back within twenty-four hours. If you need a couple of days you can say you're headed to Hong Kong. This will only be believable if you talk about this very early on. Other excuses include: interesting interviews in another city; going to meet a friend from home who will be in town for a short time; doing some activities that she can't do such as scuba or very long distance mountain biking; and checking out a real estate or business opportunity your friend has told you about.

8) Don't be afraid to admit that you masturbate. Some girls are really crazy and they can tell if you've been "active" by inspecting your happy donation. I wouldn't bring this up if it wasn't common, but it is. I'd rather have to admit that I took care of myself than have my lady think I am getting taken care of by other women.

9) Other than Bangkok, no city in Thailand is too big for a suspicious girlfriend not to be able to find you while you are picking up a bar girl. It's also easy to get spotted by one of her friends or family members. Make sure you go to places that have walls (lot of bars don't) or that are at least not on the main pay-for-play section of town.

10) Delete your history on any internet browsers you use. If women actually got a good look at the things we read about or look at on the internet they may not think about us in the same way even if we're not cheating.

11) Don't let your ladies of the night take pictures of you and don't post pictures of you and other women on Facebook or any other type of social media. Whether a girl puts pictures of you on her Facebook account or you do of her, there is a chance your lady or someone she knows can find them.

12) Don't give your phone number out,; this can only lead to trouble if you have a girlfriend. You can take phone numbers if you need to. In your phone book I suggest you name the girls with guy names, as twisted as that seems.

13) If you like the occasional happy-ending massage, make sure that your wife or girlfriend knows that you have an activity such as the gym that takes you about an hour a few times per week. I have had my gym stuff sitting in the corner of a massage room quite a few times. Just make sure you don't come back smelling like oil if she's waiting for you.

14) If you're headed home and your wife or girlfriend is there you want to make sure that you don't smell like a girl, but you also want to make sure that you don't smell like a fresh shower if it wouldn't make sense to have showered when you tell her your excuse for where you were. If you have just obviously taken a shower, she'll know something is up. The key is to clean yourself without showering yourself from top to bottom.

15) Watch your money and keep big bills hidden within your wallet. When you go to an ATM to take 10,000 baht out and two days later you need to go again, your girlfriend has a right to be suspicious and ask, "Where did that 10,000 baht go?" At the very least have some good excuses prepared for what the money was spent on, but it'll serve you well to keep her guessing instead of her having an inventory of what's in your wallet at all times.

Interestingly enough, some men use some of the tactics above to find dirt on their girlfriends, with the most typical mistake a girl makes being that she doesn't think you can read Thai. You can't but you can copy and paste into a translator or you can take a picture and have someone bilingual take a look; it works both ways. Bar girls are really hard to cheat on, harder than the average Western girl. They may think you're cheating even if you're not. If she's suspicious and she thinks something is up, it can get bad so you might almost be better off making an arrangement where she knows that from time to time you're going to meet people. As long as she knows that you always use condoms and you never see the same girl twice, she may let this go. If you're with a non-bar girl I just would never admit to anything unless I was caught red handed. They're not out to get you or catch you anyway, so I would just keep playing it smooth with them.

How to end it

You're relationship has soured and you want to end it, but you're worried about the consequences

This isn't a problem if you don't live in Thailand. You just say goodbye and it's over. But unfortunately if you live in Thailand and you've been with a girl for a while, it might not be easy for you to end it. If the girl was in a bar before, she will complain about how she has no job thanks to you, and she has no way to support herself while she finds one. She'll make it like you set her back, and she might know a couple of bad characters from her work days that would be willing to intervene on her behalf. This is why it's crucial that you have some sort of severance package set aside for her. Money will buy you out of this problem, like it will many others here. The amount of money would depend on the length of time you spent with her. If we're talking about six months or more I'd give her 20,000 baht. You tell her that you have run out of money and this is most of what you have left. It's so that she can go rent an apartment and eat while she finds a new job/bar. But before you actually give it to her you make sure she confirms that this is acceptable to her and that there will be no problems afterwards. If she complains, tell her that you could always give her 0, but that you care about her and are giving her practically all of the extra cash you have. She'll pick 20,000 baht over 0 every time.

If it's a non-bar girl that you are breaking up with, it's not her vengeance you need to worry about; it's her brothers and/or her father. You took their little girl and didn't marry her and now she's tainted forever. It's a different problem from that with the bar girl, but it has the same solution. Just tell her that you are very mentally sick right now and you will be a terrible boyfriend or husband. Then give her 20,000 baht and tell her it's just about everything you have left and you want her to use it to help find her footing from here on out. Again, it's non-negotiable and you can give 0 if they don't like 20,000. They'll take 20,000 in the end.

This all may sound unnecessary, but in analyzing problems farang have run into in the past, this one seems to come up again and again. You want to avoid major problems at all costs really, and the going rate of 20,000 baht is well worth the risks involved.

Chapter 7: THE ULTIMATE HOLIDAY/VACATION

Pick a destination

Don't bite off more than you can chew. About the only way you can mess this up is if you try to do too much and book everything in advance, thus eliminating your flexibility once you arrive. You have to fly in through Bangkok, so you might as well spend a night or two there. From there if you would like to go to the most beautiful and exotic beaches, then you can get a plane ticket to Phuket and you can visit some nearby islands once you're down there. If you're just interested mainly in nightly partners, take a bus or taxi from Bangkok to Pattaya. From Pattaya you can go to Koh Larn for a day because it's a twenty-minute boat ride, or you can take a shuttle van to Koh Chang for a couple of days, which is a great island about four hours away. If you're not a beach person and you want to see waterfalls and the country, you'll want to head north for Chiang Mai. I discuss these locations and others more in depth in Chapter 13. For your first vacation here, I would do one of the following pairs: Bangkok and Pattaya, Bangkok and Phuket, or Bangkok and Chiang Mai. And again, once you're in Pattaya you can check out an island, and if you're in Phuket you can go to another gorgeous nearby island as well.

Book a flight

First you'll need to decide when you would like to come. The peak season is more expensive but the beaches in many areas are the most beautiful during that time. If you're not coming for the beaches then you can come off-peak and save a bit. If you are headed to the southern part of the country to see the best beaches, you don't have to be in a rush to purchase your connecting flight from Bangkok. It's not likely going to save you money that way and you might enjoy the flexibility of winging it once you get to Bangkok.

Flight prices have been trending up, but oil prices play a role. Of course it seems like the prices immediately go up when oil prices do, but don't come down at all once oil prices go down. Not much you can do about that. When Japan had its tsunami, connectors through Tokyo became very cheap on the way to Bangkok, and when India is in its hottest season of the year, connectors through Delhi become cheap as well. If you're coming to Thailand you should stay for ten days or two weeks minimum if you can, and since there is a massive time difference you don't have to time it out to touch down in Bangkok in the morning like you would with some other destinations. My advice when picking your flight is to just go with the cheapest, even if you have two layovers. Using a site like Orbitz or Expedia, you should be able to find something at a decent price if you're willing to do the layovers. Travel agents usually give the worst prices, and buying straight from the airline's website is becoming more of a competitive option. The airlines like to avoid the third-party commission, so when you find a good itinerary on a site like Orbitz, you may want to check that airline's site or even give them a call to see if they can give you the same flights cheaper. This was never the case for a decade, but it works from time to time now.

Hotels

You're better off not booking anything in advance. And if you just can't bear the thought of not having a place to stay the first night you get there, then just book that one night and take care of the rest when you get in. Unlike in the West, many hotels in Thailand are more expensive if you book online than if you go in person. There is only one website I would book a hotel through and that's listed in Chapter 17. If you go on hotels.com you'll swear that Thailand is expensive for hotels, but if you just walk around and ask at the hotel lobbies you're bound to find an amazing price in the area you would like to stay. By not booking in advance you are also welcome to travel around Thailand as you please. No matter where you are you're bound to see a plethora of signs for "500 baht per

night hotel rooms." Usually they'll let you take a look at a room before you take it for the night just to make sure it's to your standards. If you use this approach and you're willing to spend 1,000 baht you'll get a nice room in every city in Thailand. Never book a hotel through a travel agent in Thailand. In these cases you will overpay for a room that will disappoint you.

Tours

I have nothing against day tours, and I actually think they are great for a variety of activities. I do recommend against any front-to-back vacation tours that take any longer than a day. In these situations you always overpay and you get stuck with a group you may not love and an agenda you might want to change. When you're in Thailand it's easy for your vacation's outlook to change if you meet someone. Play things by ear and do day tours; you can't lose that way. In Chapter 17 I give you some day-tour ideas, but a quick Google search for the activity and the location will turn up many results. Trip Advisor has reviews and if you're staying in a hotel they'll usually be able to set a tour up for you where you'll get picked up from the lobby.

Check list

You should leave your dressy clothing at home; a polo shirt and slacks is suitable for the fanciest of establishments in Thailand. Don't be that guy who had to wear a dressy button down shirt with pit stains that look like Elvis or Jesus. Here is a list of things you should bring to Thailand that you may not bring to other destinations.

1) Sun block: along with cars and certain electronics, the most overpriced item in Thailand.
2) Stomach medications and Tylenol: very different food and alcohol will cause a need.
3) Itch reliever: depending on the time of the year, mosquitoes can be a pain.
4) Hat, sunglasses, and aloe vera.
5) Sandals for the beach, sandals for dinner.
6) Shorts or cash to buy shorts when you're here.
7) Color copy of your passport: comes in handy; you don't want to take the real one everywhere.
8) Cell phone: you'll need it.
9) Never-ending supply of t-shirts and polo shirts.
10) Laptop: don't trust community computers.

Communication

Once you get here you can get a sim card with a Thai phone number for very cheap and it usually comes with minutes which you can add onto at any 7-11. Your phone will need to be unlocked for this to work. If your phone isn't unlocked you can get it unlocked anywhere in Thailand. This will usually be a fair investment as phones on eBay that are unlocked sell for more than ones that are not. If you just can't do that then you can buy a cheap phone when you get here for about 1,200 baht. You can use the phone so people back home or people in Thailand can get in touch with you. For calling out to your home country you'll be better off using Skype on your laptop. Otherwise you'll want to ask around in a cell phone shop for the best sim card for international calls to your country. Often times there is a special code to dial which allows you a decent rate. If you just dial your home phone using a basic sim without any investigation into codes and rates, you'll get gauged.

Safety First

Don't drive a motorbike unless you're experienced, and stay away from street walkers and drugs of any kind. Don't start fights for any reason; be prepared to let things go if someone (most likely a Farang) tries to start a problem with you. Don't even think anything remotely un-positive about the King or his family. Remember or keep the tourist police number, 1155, in your phone. Also, if you know you get out of control at night, pay the scariest looking guy at a Muay Thai gym to escort you for the night. Give him the money once the night is over and make sure he knows to get you out of a place if you're getting rowdy. Some people say a body guard is overdoing it and that you have issues if you need one. This is true, but many people do have issues, especially when they drink, and that doesn't stop them from booking the flight. So if you know you're going to have a wild night of drinking and you don't necessarily trust yourself, I think it makes sense to pay someone to look after you.

*Don't fight with any Thai people for any reason. Even if you're right and even if you're being asked to spend money that you shouldn't have to, always avoid a physical confrontation at any cost. I'm all for not getting taken advantage of, and some normal resistance against attempts to take advantage of you are recommended. But if you can tell that any Thai person is fuming and there is a chance of him getting physical, you need to do whatever it takes to de-fuse the situation. You may be a UFC champion, but you can't beat ten Thai men, and this is likely the situation you'd be in. When a farang and a Thai man clash, it's usually five or ten on one. Thai's aren't looking for a fight, so you'll have the opportunity to get out of one before it's too late, often just by buying a person a beer. Buying a beer or a round of beers can end nearly all fights and this is always the best way to go. You can't win here; even if you do win one on one then you might really have made an enemy who is embarrassed and then God knows what will happen. There are some farang biker gangs here and some connected Russians, so you want to avoid fights with farang too. If you and a guy on vacation fight and you win, who's to say the cops don't try and get 100,000 baht out of you while they threaten to throw you in jail? How about I just say this: **DON'T FIGHT IN THAILAND**.

Currency

Just bring big bills of your own currency and exchange them at a bank's exchange station when you arrive in Thailand. The airports always give the worst exchange rates and fees, and ATM cards get hit with 3 per cent fees in addition to charges from both banks. Big bills are changed at banks in Thailand at excellent rates, and you can't walk far without seeing an exchange center. Small bills actually get exchanged at a lower rate in many shops, so big bills are the way to go, possibly with an ATM card just as a backup. If you have baht leftover when you leave, first congratulations are in order, and second you can just exchange it on your way out, or better yet in your bank once you get home. You can also use credit cards in many places in Thailand, but you should be on guard as sneaky transaction fees are often added to bills without notice.

As a side note, the dollar and the euro are soft against the baht compared to where things were many years ago, with something like a 40 per cent drop. Some people predict that the Baht will get even stronger due to that massive debt that many European nations and the United States currently has. The prediction is that near-bankrupt countries will have to print money to pay debts, which will inflate their currencies in the process, especially against Asian currencies since China is actually the one owed trillions of dollars. Nobody is smart enough to really know will happen, but I am very comfortable with the notion that if there is massive inflation in the West, Asia will have its own problems to deal with since so many of their businesses are geared towards outsourcing to Western companies. Basically we're all tied to the hip at this point. The bottom line is that Thailand will always be a cheap place to visit and live in by comparison with our home countries, at least for our lifetimes.

Transportation in Thailand

It's very cheap to get around Thailand unless you're getting hit with the "tourist price". Tuk Tuks and motorbike taxis are very cheap but you need to agree on a price before you hop on or else you'll get nailed. Don't even say, "How much?" Tell them how much you're willing to pay and normally they'll say ok. Motor bikes are dangerous when you're driving one, but if you tell a motorbike taxi driver, "Slow" or "ChaCha", then you'll be ok since the drivers have a lot of experience. Baht buses are available in many places and usually provide the cheapest and easies transportation you can find. Regular taxi cars are the most expensive way to get around, but even they're not half as expensive as in any city you're likely from. Government buses are extremely cheap, but have a reputation for being relatively slow because of frequent stops and low top speeds. Luxury vans that shuttle a small group around are fast and cheap and usually nice inside, but the drivers often push limits in terms of speed and safety, so it's not a recommended option for someone who might be scared. I was on a luxury van to Koh Chang sitting next to a Russian couple, once. The man was a brick house and was five times as strong as me, but after an hour I could tell he was scared and I asked him if he was ok. He said, "Please make him stop!" The luxury van shuttles are certainly not for everyone. You might be tempted to rent a motorbike, but it's not recommended unless you have experience driving a motorized scooter or motorcycle. Even if you are experienced, driving in Thailand is an adjustment and figuring it out is the last thing you need to be worried about when you are on vacation. Motorbike accidents are frequent and are likely warned about in Thailand on your Embassy's website.

Pace yourself

You can get Viagra and Cialis for yourself easily if you need it; you can also drink twenty-four hours a day here, or find pay-for-play companionship at nearly twenty hours per day. Don't go too crazy. Many people lose control and get themselves overly sore or sick from too much sex or alcohol and spend half of their vacation recovering. The food situation (and how foreign food can upset your stomach easily) looms over all travellers, so don't drink like a complete fish or you'll weaken your immune system and you can get food poisoning. You'll have a better time if you don't act like it's your first Spring Break. I'd rather drink a little and have sex once a day than go absolutely off the wall for a couple of days and stare at the toilet for the rest of the trip. I wouldn't mention this if it wasn't for me seeing so many people ruin their trips simply by overdoing it.

Where are the hottest girls in town and how do I get them?

The nicest and pricier Gogos tend to have some of the hottest girls out there. This is your best bet and you can read about how to handle yourself in the establishments and with the ladies in Chapters 3 and 5. There are escort websites as well with some of the best looking girls in town, but expect Western prices. Some of the most beautiful women in Thailand don't even think about working in a bar, and you might see them working in a department store or walking around a university. Do not try and solicit these women like prostitutes, you can try to talk to them and ask them out on a date, but don't expect them to put out anytime soon.

Things to do on a dream vacation other than females

Thailand has a lot to offer other than wonderful companions. It's well known for having some of the best food in the world, so you should enjoy the food and its prices no matter where in Thailand you go. Some of the Buddhist temples are like nothing you've ever seen before. With breathtaking views all over the country, there are many places that are ideal for walking, hiking, and taking pictures. Waterfalls and beaches are obviously very popular, but if you're into more sporty activities you'll likely find an endless amount of affordable options including:

1) Windsurfing
2) Parasailing
3) Hiking
4) Kayaking
5) Golfing
6) Snorkeling/Scuba
7) Elephant Trek
8) Rafting
9) ATV
10) Mountain Biking

People interested in body art usually don't leave without a permanent reminder of their vacation since Thailand has great and dirt-cheap tattoo parlors. There are some exotic shows that involve ping pong balls that might be of interest to you since you won't get the chance to see them at home.

Jungle tours are safe and are usually a big hit. You can take a Thai cooking class or do a few Muay Thai lessons for very cheap as well, and you'll have a blast. You can also go see a night full of Muay Thai fights most weekends, depending on the city you're in. Traditional Thai massage is likely better than anything you can get at home and for a fraction of the cost. Some people come to Thailand with one suitcase and go home with two because the shopping, especially in Bangkok, is unreal. Clothing prices cannot be beat and the quality is usually better than typical items from China. Plastic surgery, including hair transplants, is extremely cheap and it's not difficult to find highly recommended and qualified doctors for the procedures.

Traps/ Scams

Thailand is generally very tourist-friendly as the economy would take a severe hit without this industry. However, to some, you're a target, especially if you make it obvious that you're on your first vacation here. Here are the most common ways people spend more than they need to, or get themselves into jams.

1) Don't use any service unless you establish the price and the terms before starting. This is for ladies, taxis, massage, and just about anything you can think of. When you let them come up with a price after the service has been given you are opening yourself up to being charged anything that person sees fit.
2) Don't rent a wave runner. I know it's tempting but there is an age-old scam here whereby they give you a wave runner that has a little damage and they make you pay an outrageous price for that damage after you're finished. People lose as much as 60,000 baht by this scam and the police tend to side with the Thais when it comes to this situation.
3) If you rent a motorbike, make sure it's from a company that is reputable and fairly large. There is another scam here where they rent you the bike and you tell them what hotel you're staying at. They use a spare set of keys to take their bike back and charge you 50,000 baht for losing it. You don't have many options if something like this happens to you.
4) If you want to buy anything that isn't from a large chain store, such as Big C or McDonald's, you should have your Thai girlfriend do the negotiating, and if possible you shouldn't even stand next to her during the process. And you should try and negotiate just about everything.
5) Don't trust the internet shops. Bring your own laptop to one if you need to. Some shops have software that records everything you do and will capture your passwords.
6) If you're in a bar or karaoke in Bangkok and someone tells you that if you go upstairs you'll see better ladies, do not go. You'll get hit with a bill that is ten times what you expect.
7) Don't use an ATM unless it's in a prominent location such as a bank, a 7-11, or a Big C.
8) You can buy up-marketcologne and designer shirts from vendors as long as you fully understand that they are completely fake.
9) Don't take a survey; it's just someone trying to trap you into a time-share tour.
10) Hold onto your wallet in any busy place and remember that there are some little children that are highly trained in the art of pick-pocketing.
11) If a baht bus is driving you fast and going completely in the wrong direction, jump out when it stops at a light or a stop sign. There have been some fake baht busses that pick up a farang and then take him some place remote and rob him.
12) Don't let your passport out of your sight; they're worth 100,000 baht on the black market so that qualifies as motivation for many.

13) Beware of someone who is going way out of their way to help you with everything, knowing you are totally new to Thailand. They are most likely looking for a handout and may cause you some problems.
14) Memory sticks are known for having far less memory than labeled.
15) Fake Viagra and Cialis are common.
16) Don't buy a suit from one of the Indian tailors. The quality will be terrible and you'll waste your money.
17) If you're offered gems or rare stones, do not think you're getting some kind of amazing deal. You're likely just getting a fake piece of jewelry. There are some legitimate shops that sell diamonds and other stones in Thailand, and they are usually more expensive than the shops in your home town.
18) Taxi drivers have deals worked out with shops and Gogo's. They get paid if they take you there, so don't trust a taxi driver if they tell you they're taking you to "the best place in town".
19) Drinks at bars are not free. If someone gives one to you for free then this is highly suspicious. Roofy attacks happen from time to time so buy your own drinks.
20) Border and airport duty-free shops have been hot spots for complaining tourists who say they've been victims. At the borders, such as in Laos, shop owners may tell you that it's fine to bring food or alcohol products through the border back to Thailand, but this turns out to be false. And at the airport duty-free, there have been many reported cases of foreigners apparently stealing items that don't make much sense and getting hefty on-the-spot fines for doing this.

You're going back home… Don't freak out

The day you're headed back home probably won't be one of your better days, but that is typical of any vacation. The difference I find in Thailand is that many men do something totally irrational as their trip is coming to a close, such as profess their love to a bar girl, buy a timeshare, or extend their trip by two weeks, putting their home-employment situation at risk . Thailand isn't going anywhere; you'll be back again soon if you plan things properly. I find that most people are very capable of coming two or three times per year if they eliminate some silly things they do in their country, like taking weekend vacations to expensive and boring places near their home. I'll also repeat something I mentioned earlier: if you think you have fallen in love with a bar girl, make sure you leave time to see another girl at the very end of your trip, just so you level your head before you come back. If you love it that much, you can most likely retire here eventually, so that is something some folks can hang their hat on.

Chapter 8: GENERAL MONEY SAVING TIPS FOR EVERYONE

1) Eat Thai food and only food that comes from Thailand
There is a temptation to go with what you know, but you should train yourself to resist this when it comes to food. Western food and Western brands come at a premium in Thailand, while Thai food is just ridiculously cheap. Even if you go to supermarkets, make sure you pick up Thailand brands to avoid bloated import costs. Some people are scared to eat from the carts but I suggest getting over this fear. Yes, one out of fifty carts sell insects. But that leaves forty-nine out of fifty carts that sell exotic Thai food for dirt-cheap. The carts tend to use less sauce, salt, and MSG than the restaurants, thus making them the superior option in terms of health and cost.

2) Don't use travel agents
Avoid any Thai travel agents, except for domestic Thai flights and shuttle van service. Travel agents can help you to find cheap travel methods within Thailand without much of a premium, so there isn't any issue when it comes to that. But booking hotels, tours, and international flights through a Thai Travel agent will result in you paying a hefty and unnecessary premium.

3) Negotiate everything with everyone
Street vendors, monthly rentals, shops, and even food vendors might try and charge a "Farang Tax." Don't just accept it, make sure you are paying the same as a Thai person would and try to bargain with anyone if it seems practical.

4) Find flea markets and Thai markets
Many cities have flea markets with vendors selling all types of interesting products. They're a great

place to buy gifts for your family back home, or to let your Thai girlfriend pick out a few nice things. You can also find clothing for yourself at amazing prices. Nothing at the flea markets is expensive and you can always get the vendors down on price. It's a fun activity with your girlfriend, just beware of pick-pockets.

5) Don't overlook 7-11
Convenience stores in the West sell everything at a huge markup compared to large big-box stores such as Wal-Mart, as you pay extra for the convenience. This isn't the case in Thailand, and the 7-11 you can walk to will usually have competitive prices with the big box stores such as Big C. Avoiding transportation fees, you might end up saving money at a 7-11.

6) Pay-as-you-go data plans

Pre-paid sim cards are great as long as you aren't using them for long-distance calls. But even better are the pre-paid data plans you can add to your sim card (1-2 Call offers this). It comes out to something like 100 baht for 30 hours of internet use on your phone. The key is to know how to turn the internet and gps functionality on and off completely. Your phone probably has Wifi so you never need to burn data minutes when you are home. As long as you can remember to turn the internet off when you're home and when you're not using it, it'll cost you around 200 baht per month to use full internet on your phone for 50+ hours which should be more than enough. If you just want to check your email, turn it on and take a look before turning it off.

7) Skype

Before you come to Thailand, make sure you sign up for an unlimited subscription to talk to anyone from your home country for free for one year. This is usually about 900 baht for the year. If you try and do this once you are in Asia you'll find it impossible as the subscriptions can only be bought when you're home. For an additional 900 baht per year, Skype will even give you a phone number that people will see when you call them and that they'll be able to call you on anytime at no charge to you. This feature includes voicemail service. With a Skype application on your cell phone you'll really be rocking and rolling. Between Skype and a prepaid data plan, I have a highly functional communication system down to an incredibly low price each month.

8) Walking is good for you

I constantly see foreign men using some type of transportation service while I see Thai people happily walking. You eventually get used to the heat and walking is good for you. Why not walk whenever possible instead of spending money and getting no exercise?

9) One island or exotic location is probably enough

I have "island-hopped" many times in Thailand and my experience has taught me one thing, one fantastic island is usually pretty much the same as another. If you have a great island near where you are staying or living, frequent that place instead of feeling compelled to visit every single island you've never been to. Avoiding extra travel time should make for a better all-round experience and you'll save good money over time. Also keep in mind that any island will be more expensive for basic things than inland as there are extra fees for the deliveries from the mainland.

10) Don't drink at Western-style pubs

Drinking at the Irish pubs or Western-style restaurants will come with hefty tabs. It's tempting, but a good buzz is a good buzz. Who needs air conditioning when you're drinking cold beers anyhow?

11) Watch TV for free

Everything depends on you having a strong internet connection wherever you are staying. With this you can watch almost anything for free online. Vuze and Hulu give you tons of free content and a quick Google search will result in dozens of options for watching new episodes of your favorite TV shows. It's also easy enough to find free movies, or you can get an online package for Netflix if you're not against paying. I literally watch every episode of every television show that I like within twelve hours of when it airs and in perfect quality with no exceptions, all for free. I can also see just about every movie as well. With entertainment options becoming more and more online, going international no longer means that you have to downgrade your home entertainment. Actually, you'll likely increase the options you have and decrease the price by 90 per cent. And nobody is watching this stuff from their tiny laptop screen; you can easily connect your laptop to any television. Then just buy a wireless keyboard and mouse. I am literally typing this out from my wireless keyboard on my coffee table looking at my television monitor. My eyes have thanked me for this! I also have an online Sirius Satellite subscription which gives me incredible radio, 24-7.

12) Don't miss out on deals that Thais get, such as coupons, movie deals etc.
There are coupons and deals in Thailand, but they're written in Thai, so foreigners never take advantage of them. Even in 7-11 there are sale items scattered around and it's a total waste to most. Don't overlook the savings as they can be significant over time. You can have your Thai friend or companion do some translating for you or you can check out the application for your cell phone called "Google Goggles". This lets you take a picture of anything and it will translate it into English for you. In one restaurant I go to they have a section in English and a section in Thai; the prices are different for the same items! I use Google Goggles and I order from the Thai part of their menu to get the same prices as the natives. I also notice that many large stores, chains and even movie theatres are obviously reaching out to foreign customers with some of their advertisements, but their sales and discounts are only written in Thai. Make sure you're paying the Thai price for things and don't overlook coupons and even "half of movie night".

13) Find an all-in-one gym club that has a pool and other amenities; you'll get your money's worth.
If you aren't staying at a resort, you're saving a lot of money every day but you probably don't have a nice pool or gym to use. You can find a nearby gym/club that has everything you could possibly need, probably for about 200 baht per day. One-month, six-month, and annual membership fees are usually extremely affordable.

14) If there are vendors or peddlers only trying to sell to foreigners, skip it.
If you see someone selling only to foreigners, they are doing so because they know that Thai people won't fall for the same tricks or inflated prices. A perfect example is some of the vendors who sell boat tours to "the island". They never solicit Thai people but will harass almost any farang they see. Most of the time they're just charging you double or triple for the same ticket you can buy from the main dock point.

15) There's almost always a better and cheaper place to stay.
Whether you live here or are staying for a short while, there is almost always a similar place to stay for a much cheaper rate. Give yourself a few hours to walk around and take a look at places and prices, and if you have a Thai speaker with you this will help. Rents and hotel rates in Thailand are amazingly cheap if you avoid the most tourist-friendly locations. If you're willing to walk an extra block or two to the beach or the main street, you may save a significant amount daily or monthly. If you're really on a budget you can get down to 300 baht per day for a half-way decent place, or 3,000 for a month.

16) Gogos lower their prices after a certain time (some of them do, anyway).
In many places, 1am is the cut-off and when the bar fine gets sliced by 50 per cent. Going to a Gogo early gives you first pick, and going late gets you a discount in many establishments, which means that going at 11:30 gets you nothing good.

17) Make deals or arrangements with bar girls/Gogo girls.
Girls will give you discounts if you work around their schedule. If they know they can see you once they finish their shift at a bar then they'll give you a break if you arrange such a thing ahead of time.

You become their safety net in case they can't find a long-time customer for the evening. You'll get a cheaper price and you'll avoid the bar fine without having to pay for dinners, tips, or even drinks.

18) Buy a motorbike from an auction

I noticed that the used-bike shops are selling scooters and motorbikes that are a year old for 80-90 per cent of the original price. This would never fly at home because of significant depreciation. For whatever reason, cars and bikes just don't depreciate the same here, even though bikes typically don't last too long. I think getting a used bike for a minimal discount is crazy, so I decided to find out where these shops are getting their bikes, and I found that they buy them from auctions. All the big cities have auctions where repossessed motorbikes are for sale for extremely reasonable prices, and the auctions are open to the public.

19) Come off-peak

Late April to mid-November will give you the best prices on flights, hotels, and even women.

20) Don't over-tip or tip at all in some situations

I cover this more in depth in the FAQ, but tipping is strange in Thailand, and it's tough to ever really know what is appropriate. Oftentimes, 0 is the most appropriate, so when in doubt I suppose you'll save some baht. And remember that, traditionally, Thailand is a non-tipping country.

21) Find the right ATM

If you have to take cash out, find the ATMs that let you take 20,000 baht out so that you aren't getting hit with fees twice as often you would on machines that have a 10,000-baht limit.

22) Pick the right place to visit

Koh Samuit and Phuket are very expensive. Pattaya and Bangkok are cheaper, but if you're really on a budget you can do much better in places like Chiang Mai.

23) Water and the right alcohol

Soft drinks are unhealthy and they're a waste of money. Drink water, and if you want to drink beer, stick to the Thai beers which are fresh and cheap. For hard alcohol, Thai whisky is dirt-cheap, but you should avoid the very lowest quality whiskies as you'll pay in other ways for drinking them.

24) Air Conditioning

Your body will adjust to the weather and the conditions of using only a fan if it needs to. It might be a rough transition for you in the beginning, but after a while you'll get used to it. Or at the very least, try and use the AC as sparingly as possible.

One interesting tip regarding AC units is to not rule out renting a place because it doesn't have one. You'll usually get a discount on a place if there is no AC, and then you can just buy a cheap unit that you can take with you to future residences.

25) Stock up on items before you stay in a resort or island hotel.

If you're going to an island where you probably won't leave your hotel or resort much, if at all, make sure you load up on water and snacks before you reach your destination. You'll save potentially a few thousand baht by doing this.

Chapter 9: LIVING IN THAILAND

Why?

For some folks, a permanent move to Thailand isn't possible. Between their family and career responsibilities, they just can't go half way around the world for good. If you don't have children or your children are out of the house, you stand a much better chance of being able to make this happen. Also, since a good income in Thailand is hard to come by, those with a significant amount of retirement savings will be in a much better position to do this. But why would someone who has savings and does not have young children want to move to Thailand? Why wouldn't they?

With costs in your home country spiraling out of control, the cost of living in Thailand is extremely tempting. Unless you live in Hawaii, you probably don't live in a place that can compete with the weather or the natural beauty of Thailand either. Amazing food, amazing and available women, and a bevy of things to do help to make Thailand a premier place to live for those who have the financial and family flexibility to make it happen.

Certainly it can be different for those who are not close to retirement age compared to those who are approaching the milestone. If you don't have a considerable amount of money saved up then you'll find it hard to ever get to that point living in Thailand. I'll go over some key positives and negatives for people who fit into both of these categories, and some will obviously be redundant.

Advantages of living in Thailand for those not close to retirement age:

-Severe drop in cost of living.
-Opportunities with women that don't even come close to existing back home.
-Much better chance to have a healthy and happy relationship with a woman.
-Will likely jump-start an active night/social life.
-Amazing weather and incredible beauty throughout Thailand.
-Environment conducive to being as healthy as can be (food, weather, and free time for gym).
-Much less-stressful environment should help short- and long-term health as well as happiness levels.
-More available/affordable hobbies and activities.
-Weekly work will be much easier, one way or another.
-Will have an amazing time whenever any friends or family members visit you.
-Recent internet technology advances make staying in touch with friends easy.
-Recent internet technology advances mean home entertainment options won't skip a beat.
-Starting a family in Thailand is much easier, and the odds of having a happy family are good.
-Cleaning, laundry, house-maintenance are almost non-factors in terms of cost.

Disadvantages of living in Thailand for those not close to retirement age:

-Will not spend time with friends and family and it will be difficult for people to visit you.
-Each year spent away from home will make it harder to ever re-join the work force if you had to.
-You will make significantly less money each month in Thailand.
-You may be spending your peak work-years in a location where you can't make good money.
-You may not be able to save enough for retirement, especially if you ever wanted to live back home.
-You could start to lose some of your verbal and other skills because you may not be using them often.
-If you're under 50, you'll have some visa issues from time to time.
-Temptations loom, that weak minded or people with addictive personalities can fall victim to.
-You'll have trouble truly owning a home.

Advantages of living in Thailand for those close to retirement age:

-Whatever your target total-net-worth to retire on was, you can probably cut that in half or less.
-Will be able to pay for and maintain a larger/nicer place to live, almost without exception.
-Ten times the opportunities with women that don't even come close to existing back home.
-Much better chance to have a healthy and happy relationship with a woman.
-Will likely jump-start an active night/social life.
-Amazing weather and incredible beauty throughout Thailand.
-Environment conducive to great health (food, weather, and free time for gym).

-Much less stressful environment should help short- and long-term health, as well as happiness levels.
-More available/affordable hobbies and activities.
-Your friends probably have the financial means to visit you more than they would if you were younger.
-Recent internet technology advances make staying in touch with friends easy.
-Recent internet technology advances mean home entertainment options won't skip a beat.
-Cleaning, laundry, house maintenance are almost non-factors in terms of cost.
-Costs of medical care and medicine are as low as can be.
-Pension and/or social security will likely pay for all of your bills here with room to spare while...
-Interest on your savings can provide you with a high budget for entertainment and domestic travel.
-Will find it easy to meet people and make friends as there are many retirees who live here.

Disadvantages of living in Thailand for those close to retirement age:

-Will not be able to visit children and grandchildren often.
-Will have to adjust to a whole new world.
-Opportunities for side businesses and part time jobs will be almost non-existent.
-You'll have trouble truly owning a home.

*It's a short list; it makes a lot of sense to retire in Thailand right now, even if you're married.

That leaves very young people, such as those from 18 to 25. If you're in that age bracket and you just want to travel and see the world without having any concerns for future, career, or retirement savings, then I think Thailand would make a great place for about a year if you can manage to find a teaching job during that time.

Retiring in Thailand doesn't require an enormous amount of money, especially if you have some sort of working pension or future government pension to supplement your spending. As beautiful and wild a place as it is, I think it is an ideal retirement spot for single or divorced men, and I think it will catch on more and more as an "early retirement" haven. So for those who have some equity in their house, and a retirement fund, and are maybe 10 or even 15 years away from being able to retire in their own country, they may be able to quit and head to Thailand right now, and who could blame them?

For people that don't have any substantial savings and won't have a suitable pension coming in for quite a while, if ever, it's not impossible to make it in Thailand, but it's difficult. If you have a degree you stand a much better chance of getting a decent-paying job allowing you to live very comfortably. The issue is that you would never make enough money to save much for retirement. But if you are due to get a nice government pension one day and you're frugal enough to at least save something every month, then you should be ok down the road in Thailand since it will always be fairly inexpensive to live in many nice areas. Without a degree and without much savings, you might not be ready to move to Thailand unless you are guaranteed some sort of inheritance once day, or you have some sort of residual or online business and you are very confident in your abilities to make money online from your home country as you live in Thailand. If you haven't already made good money online, then you shouldn't be confident.

Visa

You can't stay in Thailand without a visa; some people do this but the stress they go through is not worth any advantages of living here. People used to be able to cross borders every thirty or sixty days to keep their tourist visa going forever, but they won't let you do this long-term anymore. If you are financially capable of living here and aren't coming here with the last of your money in your pocket, you can always find a way to get a visa. You'll always spend some money and some time on it though. Also keep in mind that once you get a visa, you usually need to purchase a re-entry permit if you want to leave Thailand for a bit and still have your active visa when you come back. You can get a multiple re-entry permit if you travel frequently, and this needs to be renewed annually. Here are the available visa options:

Retirement Visa

If you're over 50, you don't have much to worry about. You can easily secure retirement visas year after year for a relatively cheap price. For a retirement visa you need to show either 800,000 baht in your bank account, OR your combined income/pension must be 65,000 baht per month or higher. If you have an income that is less than 65,000 baht and a savings of less than 800,000 baht you may still be eligible if your bank account + (income X 12) = 800,000 baht. If you don't qualify in any of those three areas you aren't financially suited to retire here anyway, so the rules are fair in my opinion. You can expect to spend about 20,000 baht per year (including the lawyer's fee) to maintain your visa, and the work load will be light. You'll have to show up to a place a few times per year to keep the Thai government updated on your contact information, and once a year your lawyer will have to resubmit your paperwork. You're looking at twenty minutes of work and hassle four times per year plus 20,000 baht per year. Lastly, if you have outstanding warrants from your home country, you'll run into problems because they do check you out.

Work Permit - with Non-Immigrant Visa

If you're under 50, you can get a visa but it's not as easy as it is for the retirement visa. The easiest and cheapest way to maintain a visa here is to secure a proper work permit with a non-immigrant visa, most likely by working as a teacher. The Ministry of Education will give you a visa as long as you have a four-year degree (bachelors) and a school willing to pay you to teach. I'll expand on this more in the "working in Thailand" section of this chapter. But in a nutshell, if you have a four-year degree you'll find it easy to get a teaching job, and easy to get the visa. Without the degree you won't get the visa.

Investment Visa

If you have substantial savings and you're under 50 then you won't have a big issue, because you can get an investment visa for roughly 10 million baht. As long as you have that amount in a combination of Thai bank accounts, bonds, or real estate, you'll be granted a visa. The number goes up if you bring a spouse or children with you, by a few million baht each.

Business Visa

You can also get a business via here, but this is probably the most difficult and annoying Visa to have. You'll need to pass a long list of requirements that includes a Thai business partner, an office, all sorts of letters, and significant net worth. On top of that you'll have to spend in excess of 30,000 baht per month to keep it going. This is only an option if you really want to open a business here, and that's not an easy task. You can read more about opening a business in Thailand in Chapter 11.

Marriage Visa

A solid visa option if you have limited funds and are under 50 years old is to get married. If you marry a Thai national and you don't have a criminal background, you can get a visa going and keep it each year for about the same amount of time and money as the retirement visa. So figure on 20,000 baht each year, and you need to be able to show some combination of savings and/or income similar to retirement visa requirements, but perhaps lower (maybe even 400,000 baht in the bank).

Student Visa

This is an overlooked option for people who are relatively young but have funds and/or some type of income that comes in from their home country. You can get a student visa for around 20,000 baht per year, and classes don't cost much, if anything, on top of that. Your actual "in class time" will vary from very little to extremely little depending on the school and lawyer you find that gets you your visa. This is a good option for some.

*** I only endorse two businesses in Thailand officially, and I won't even list them in the book since this isn't ad space.

1)   If you need a very affordable and old-school match-maker in Isan to find you a beautiful non-bar girl as a long term spouse or wife, please let me know and I'll get you the details.

2)   If you're under 50 and you think you're going to run into Visa issues, I know a place that has the perfect solution.

So if you want to talk further about either of these two things, make sure you email me at: info@thaigirlspattayagirls.com

Moving to Thailand

If you've been to Thailand before, you'll have an easier time making decisions. If you haven't, you should go on a trial basis before you go and sell all of your possessions. You may need to visit a couple of locations to decide on which place you intend to call your home base. Throughout this chapter you'll read about things that should help you to decide just how feasible it will really be to do it. If it is financially practical for you to come, and you feel that the advantages outweigh the disadvantages, then I guess it's time for you to start thinking about the logistics of a move.

Certain visas give you an opportunity to move your possessions into the country tax-free, while others don't. I really don't think you should bring that much over with you in either case. If you follow my advice you will be going to Thailand without having arranged a long-term housing situation (finding one online will be double or triple the price). So your best bet is to throw out the things that you know you don't need and that have no value, sell the things that you don't need and do have value, and store the rest in a private storage. Once you finalize your residence situation in Thailand, and you have confirmed that you are going to stay here indefinitely, you can take down the storage on your next visit home and decide what to do with the items.

You'll never need winter clothing in Thailand, so it would be best if a friend could let you keep just enough winter clothing in a spare closet so you have enough to get by on if you visit during a cold season. It's a total waste to move any furniture with you, so just sell what you have on Craigslist. Many Thai houses and condos come fully furnished, and if not, Thailand has some of the most affordable furniture I have ever seen. Don't go overboard bringing clothing with you either. Bring your favorite items and your summer stuff. If you ship clothing to Thailand, you'll probably pay more than you would to buy similar items new once you get here. Remember, clothing is extremely affordable in Thailand. On your first trip out you should fill two large suitcases with everything you'll need. When you go back home to visit, take the same two suitcases back with you, but mostly empty. Then fill them up again on your way back to Thailand. Four large suitcases full of your possessions should get the job done. You can buy small items like kitchen and bathroom items very cheap in Thailand. It's really just your clothing, your smaller electronics, and your keepsakes that you want to bring with you. Actually, photos are such a burden to carry around and keep that I paid a service $150 USD to digitalize all of my photos which I now have on CDs, computer drives, and web backup. I didn't throw the pictures out (although I could at this point), but they're in a box in my best friend's basement. Nice TV's are more expensive in Thailand than they are in your home country, so you can ship or bring yours with you on the plane if it makes sense for you to do so.

You can bring a dog or a cat to Thailand with you as well. It's a little pricey and there's a whole process associated with it, but many people do it. You'd be better off bringing them with you on your second trip once everything is squared away with a proper living space and you're sure you are staying in Thailand long-term. Computers are not cheap in Thailand, so bring yours with you. The only other items I can see being worth the hassle would be golf clubs or a pricey bicycle.

Try to spend as little as possible when you first arrive. Many people often look back at their first month or two with regret because they spent significant amounts of money foolishly. After you're here for a decent amount of time, you'll have a better feel for getting the most out of your money, and you'll be in a better position to spend on things. Do yourself a favor and do not be in "vacation mode" when you arrive. You should come in "business mode", trying to carve out the best and most economical lifestyle for yourself. This will require work on your part. You'll have plenty of time to enjoy Thailand once you know your way around.

When you have picked out the location you want to live in, it's a good idea to pay someone to help you. You may need help finding a good place to rent and to negotiate rent prices. You'll also need someone to drive you around town, and to help you carry home the necessity items you buy. 700 baht for a day's worth of help is more than enough. Figure one day to help you find a place and another day to help you move into it. You should pay for their gas and for their food while they are with you, and a small bonus when you're all done should be paid as well. Some may say this is too much, but you're asking someone who speaks English fluently to quit whatever they do for two days and drive you all over; I think it's worth paying them a few hundred baht extra just to get things sorted quickly. If the person is helpful keep them happy in case you need help in the future.

House or condo hunting; renting vs. owning

Owning a home isn't easy in Thailand and you may never be able to really own a property free and clear as there are laws against foreigners owning more than 49 per cent. With condos it's different, and it makes more sense since you don't have to worry about it being taken away. Some people appreciate the privacy of living in a house, and some people enjoy the convenience of a condo. It's a matter of preference, and the city you're living in will dictate the viability of either. Relating to Thailand, I have lived in every type of property and my biggest complaint about the average apartment or condo is that the walls are not made with the same thickness as in many U.S. buildings I have lived in. With no soundproofing on the walls, the average Thai condo has privacy concerns. There are always exceptions and obviously some builders have made it more of a priority than others. I find that it's difficult to get a good deal on a condo and you're usually paying a premium to live in one. The exception is if you're living in a really cheap one where the accommodations are not close to first class. But if you want a Western-style kitchen and a nice bedroom and view, you're going to be living with mostly other ex-pats, and as such you'll be paying well above "Thai prices." It should also be noted that a real estate investment in Thailand right now isn't likely to be profitable for you. Thailand is getting past its boom, and with so many financial problems in Western countries, it seems unlikely that prices will go up anytime soon. Actually they have built too many luxury condos in some cities.

In my eyes, the best option is to rent a Thai-owned home. You can drive around town with a Thai helper or friend and you'll see many homes with signs that say, "For Rent." Have your Thai friend call the number and the first question they ask should be, "How much per month?" If it's in your budget then they'll often come to meet you right away to show you the place. They'll be surprised when they see that it's a farang who wants to rent and they'll wish they'd said a higher price. But it's too late and you already got the correct and accurate "Thai price" from them. They may actually try and tell you they made a mistake and that its higher, but you can just leave if they do that. As in any other place, there are good deals and bad deals in Thailand. Some people aren't honest with themselves about how much their property is worth, while others are desperate to have some type of income and will shoot very low to get a tenant. Aside from the fact that they may try and get more money out of you, Thais are generally happy to have farang tenants as we have a pretty good reputation for keeping things clean and repairing any damage we cause. Be prepared to pay for first, last, and security up-front. You can negotiate with them just to pay two months instead of three, but they have a point if they mention that you're a risk to leave at any time to go back home. If you find an amazing place and it just doesn't have AC, you can put in your own new unit for about 25,000 baht if you ask some AC repair men around town. That's yours to keep and you can always sell it for at least half of what you paid, or you can take it with you to the next house you live in.

You can find any type of home you're looking for in most cities and towns, from small and extremely cheap to large and still fairly cheap. I understand what it's like to own a home, and when you're renting you can't make modifications or stay indefinitely since it's not yours. However, this is not your country, so a house you buy here is never really yours anyway. Real estate agents gouge farang on prices and can't be trusted, so don't use them for renting or buying. If you spend a full day or two looking at a dozen or more homes to rent, getting the real "Thai price" on them in the process, you're going to find an amazing deal or two. You'll have a lease that'll protect you from being unexpectedly kicked out, and if you're asked to leave when the lease is up, it'll take you another couple of days to find something similar or even better. Having someone move your stuff from one house to another will be 90 per cent cheaper than it would be in your home country.

So here is a quick recap of the four options:

Buying a home:
- Can't own it 100%
- Not a great investment
- Chance you'll want to move back to your home country and lose money
- Can get something nice for very cheap

Buying a nice condo:
- Can own it 100%
- Cheaper than comparable locations in your home country, but often overpriced in Thailand
- Not a great investment
- Chance you'll want to move back to your home country and lose money
- No privacy and thin walls are common
- Can live in some excellent locations including beach front

Renting a nice condo:
- The most overpriced option in Thailand

- Excellent location very possible
- Total flexibility to leave and move
- Privacy concerns
- No investment or major up-front costs to worry about
- Usually come fully furnished

Renting a home:
- Will spend very little per month
- Privacy no concern
- Total flexibility to leave and move
- Will probably be a small distance from the hot-spots
- No investment or major up-front costs to worry about
- Usually come fully furnished

As I mentioned there is also the option of complete budget-housing available to those that need it or to those that just aren't interested in having a nice place with a Western kitchen. You can rent a room without a real bedroom for very cheap, and some are obviously better than others. Depending on the city, you can get down to 3,000 baht per month for something liveable, but again no bedroom and no kitchen. For 8,000 baht per month you can find something decent with a bedroom and some sort of kitchen in just about every city. In most places you can find a decent small home for 12,000 to 15,000, a nice, somewhat spacious home for 20,000, and a really nice house maybe with a pool for 30,000 per month. Look on the internet or use a real estate agent and you can double the prices. Koh Samuit, Phuket, and Bangkok are expensive compared to any place else.

Don't overlook my tip on house-hunting. Make sure you drive around town with your Thai helper and have them call places with for-rent signs, asking how much per month. Don't take the first one you get, and look at ten or more. Experienced ex-pats always live in a nice place for a great monthly price while rookies are usually overpaying. You should be in a good situation now to avoid the "rookie tax."

How to best use the banking system

You're looking for the lesser of evils here as there is no perfect way. With a proper Visa you can get a bank account here, but it'll pay either 0% interest or very little interest. If you deposit an international check into your account they'll charge you 1,200 baht and it takes thirty days to clear. And if you wire in money, then your bank at home will charge you. There are also fees for having a Thai debit card and even for the account itself. If you go to an ATM with your home country's debit card, your home bank will most likely charge you from 2 to 3% as a transaction fee, which can get nasty, plus the Thai bank charges you as well, usually 150 baht. So some people wire enough money to live on for six months at a time into their Thai bank. By doing this they don't make interest on that money and they pay account fees, fees to have the debit card, and fees for wiring the money.

The best option for you will depend on your budget here. So if you spend a lot of money, wiring funds every six months into a Thai bank account will wind up being the safest and the cheapest option after weighing things up. You'll lose out on interest, but the alternative would be going to the ATM every few days and getting hit with high transaction charges from two banks. It would be too costly in the end, and you couldn't benefit much from bringing cash back with you after a visit home because holding onto any more than two months' worth of spending would be too risky.

If you're not a big spender, I think it makes the most sense to avoid having a Thai bank account and to bring a stack of cash with you every time you come back from a visit home. In this case you'll also want to use your home country's debit card to make purchases whenever there is no extra fee for doing so, and you'll have no choice but to use the ATM in some situations, withdrawing the maximum of 20,000 baht each time. You'll wind up getting hit with some 2 or 3% ATM charges maybe an average of once a month, but I don't see that costing more than frequently wiring money, not making interest on the money sitting in your Thai account, and getting hit with additional account fees. If anything, it would cost around the same and it would be a whole lot easier not having to do wires or setting up and maintaining a new account. Again, what really makes this work is bringing three to four months' worth of spending cash with you each time you visit home (once per year seems to be average). If you're not a big spender, this shouldn't be such a risk and it's not like you're going to tell anyone where your hiding spot is. Some people have watches or laptops worth more sitting in their apartment.

If you're married, things change a bit; you can wire money into your wife's account and there's no extra fee or hassle other than the wire itself.

Working in Thailand

Retirees looking for extra cash should be able to make some extra money teaching English, and many do. If you're coming to Thailand and will need a job to cover your living expenses, you should be prepared for two inevitabilities: 1) You probably won't make a lot of money here 2) its not easy to find even a half-way decent job here.

To work you'll need a work permit and these are only given out if you can clearly demonstrate useful skills. If you have experience in the oil industry you'll probably be OK, and if you have a four-year degree you'll probably wind up OK as well. There are some corporate jobs here, for which companies can get you a work permit and visa without any problems, but these jobs are not common, and your resume would most likely need to be impressive and include the degree. Not speaking Thai will eliminate many such jobs. If you're fairly young, have a four-year degree, an impressive resume, and you look and talk the part of an executive, you can find a decent corporate job in Bangkok. It will take time and it won't pay more than one-third of what a similar job would pay in the West, but your spending will be one-third too, so the pay is relative. Most people just don't fit those criteria, so they have only a small chance of getting a job like that. These people eventually look to teach English.

There are a billion people in Asia trying to learn English, so any native English speaker who has some patience is a viable candidate to teach it. Unfortunately in Thailand, the Ministry of Education doesn't quite see it that way and they want you to have a four-year degree. Many people get a fake degree and fake transcripts and are able to get around the system, but they're cracking down now and you can technically do some jail time if you get caught. Fitting with a popular theme in this book, we never want to do anything that risks any jail time in Thailand because even a weekend in prison will damage us severely. The Ministry of Education and the Thai labor department make exceptions from time to time, but they're doing someone a favor when they do and you can't count on that happening for you. Getting a permit and visa without a degree will depend on how well connected the school that is hiring you is, luck, and your personal appearance. If you are well-dressed and good looking you have a much better shot; it shouldn't be that way, but it is. There are many people who get some type of visa such as a marriage visa, and then they teach without a work permit. Schools are desperate for teachers in some areas and they'll employ you even if you're not totally legit, but they won't pay you the same wages and you'll have no real rights should something bad happen. The bottom line is, if you don't have a degree and you want to teach in Thailand, it's possible but you have major disadvantages, including lower pay, few options of where you can teach, and visa issues.

If you do have a bachelor's degree you'll be able to find employment as a teacher. You should look into teaching courses such as TEFL. Generally, the paper that says you have completed the course is all you're after, so avoid the more expensive TEFL courses that make empty promises. Once you are certified you can begin hunting for a job on the Ajarn.com website. Bangkok opportunities are the most abundant and usually offer the best salaries. If you turn out to be a good and patient teacher in Bangkok you can actually make a good salary, and there are easy overtime opportunities available as well, although you'll want to make sure your contract allows for it. Most qualified teachers start at just over 30,000 baht per month, but many teachers in or near Bangkok make close to 60,000 or even more. Anyone can live well in Thailand on 60,000 baht or more, and 30,000 would work as long as you have some type of savings and/or investments.

Teaching really should be more of a natural fit in Thailand. There is a shortage of teachers, and how many highly qualified four-year degree-holding Westerners can just pick up and move half way around the world? They should lessen the requirements so that anyone with a clean background and a resume that shows some type of work history should be able to get a job. Then it would be up to the schools to hire those they feel do the best in the interview process. If you don't have a degree and your dream is to teach at a decent-enough salary in Thailand, you should try and get the easiest and most affordable four-year degree you can get, even if it takes some time. There are accredited online schools that can give you a degree, just make sure it's a real school.

Teaching isn't for everyone, and depending on your school you may face some very difficult teenagers to work with. Most of your students won't care about your lesson plans and they won't do homework. They may even cause constant disruptions or even curse you out. This happens in certain cities all over the world, and it tends to be a difficult and underpaid profession in any country. You may also not like how you are treated by your boss, and half of the schools or more don't have proper air conditioning. Teaching works well for some in Thailand, but there are many people who hate teaching here who do it because it's the only thing they can do. Without a good salary, I don't see an unhappy teacher's quality of life being any higher than it would be if they were home, and it might be worse or significantly worse.

I'm not sugar-coating it because what good would that do? If you're the type who can get a decent corporate job in Bangkok, you're the type who can probably get a good job anywhere. If you have a degree and you truly believe you'll find teaching in Thailand to be rewarding, you can carve out a nice lifestyle for yourself here. If you don't have a degree and you're willing to teach for a little less than what it will take to live a nice lifestyle thanks to a significant savings or side-income, then you'll be fine. If you have no substantial savings or side-income/pension, and no degree, you aren't ready to move to Thailand permanently.

Cost of Living Breakdown with quality of life discussion at every level

Some cities are more expensive than others, and islands are particularly so. If you're ok living in the middle of nowhere you can get by on peanuts, but I doubt that would be a fulfilling life. I know many of you want to see a cost-of-living breakdown and I am going to give that to you, but you have to keep this in mind: I'm giving you the average. Chiang Mai and even some nice but quiet beach towns can be cheaper, while Phuket and Koh Samuit are more expensive. Bangkok is slightly  higher than average unless you want to have a spacious place to live, in which case the costs sky-rocket. Pattaya is very average unless you let temptations get in the way of your budget. Here are a few hypothetical examples of some working budgets in Thailand with in-depth descriptions of each according lifestyle. Keep in mind that the men in the hypothetical situations have read this book and take advantage of many of the money-saving strategies. Also keep in mind that in your first month you'll have to pay some deposits and you'll have to buy some basic-need items. You'll probably spend twice your monthly budget in that first month, not including your one-way flight.

Bob, a 30-year-old with a small savings who teaches English for 30,000 baht per month

Apartment	4,000 baht per month
Electric	500 baht per month
Bank fees	600 baht per month
Phone	300 baht per month
Internet	600 baht per month
Food	5,000 baht per month
Miscellaneous	3,000 baht per month
Savings	3,000 baht per month
Entertainment	10,000 baht per month
Visit-home fund	3,000 baht per month
Total	30,000 baht per month

Bob gives a lot of people hope as he lives a simple but decent life on a modest 30,000 baht per month, which at the present time comes to $983 USD or 693 euro. Bob lives in a small, one-room apartment with just enough kitchen equipment to get by and a good-enough bed, TV, and desk area with a small table and chair set to eat, or for his friends to sit on. He only uses AC for an average of thirty minutes per day as he has adjusted to using just a fan. He used my tricks for TV, Internet, and phone so he is at no loss when it comes to those things. He eats a good diet of local Thai food and goes to small, Thai eateries and food carts from time to time. At 100 baht per day for miscellaneous he has enough to get a haircut twice per month and to get the cheap brands on things like toilet paper, hair products, tooth paste, and laundry detergent. He cleans his own clothing and his apartment. If Bob is an American his "visit-home fund" lets him go back every fifteen months, and if he's from Europe he'll be able to visit every year. His 36,000-baht-per-year savings will not amount to much and may provide more of a "large purchase fund" for thing like phones, computers, a doctor's bill and motorbikes he'll need in the future. He's young enough so he doesn't worry about health insurance, and he exercises in his apartment to save money.

With 10,000 baht per month in entertainment, Bob has more than enough to buy his girlfriend the occasional bouquet of flowers, or take her out to movies, dinners, bowling, and the beach a few times per week. He can enjoy the occasional local brew from time to time as well. When Bob is single he can spend his entertainment money on one or two girls per week but he won't be seen in a Gogo. As I mentioned in bold at the top, Bob has a "small savings." He can't tap into it to supplement his salary because the compound interest the savings makes is the only shot he has of being able to retire one day, since he isn't able to save much from year to year. He always has companionship but he never has luxury. He doesn't worry about bills, and Thailand provides him with plenty of free activities, such as hiking. He stays connected by going home every year and chatting on the internet. He simply doesn't have the room in his budget to get married and have a family, but Bob is fine with that, at least for now. The strict budget can be annoying, but Bob has learned to live without things that some Westerners think are necessary. It's not a bad way to live, and we can see how Bob enjoys the simplicity of it all, but we also see Bob changing his mind about a few things in about eight years, namely having a family. All-in-all, Bob is probably less stressed and happier than many overstressed and slightly depressed people from his country, but we're not about to be foolish enough to say that Bob is living the dream. He's made sacrifices to enjoy an easy, simple life. Surely there are people out there who would trade places with Bob, and surely there are people who wouldn't.

Jim, a 60-year-old who has 6,000,000 baht in savings, receives 20,000 baht as some type of pension, and has no additional income or work of any kind.

Rent	8,000 baht per month
Electric	900 baht per month
Bank fees	900 baht per month
Phone	300 baht per month
Internet	600 baht per month
Food	6,000 baht per month
Miscellaneous	5,200 baht per month
Entertainment	15,000 baht per month
Visit-home fund	3,000 baht per month
Health related	4,500 baht per month
Gym club	600 baht per month
Total	45,000 baht per month

Jim gives hope to people who haven't been able to strike it rich on real estate or save a lot of money over time, thanks to living an active early retirement in a place where he can easily meet women.

With 6,000,000 baht in savings ($200,000 USD or 140,00 euro) I'm figuring that Jim can spend 5 per cent a year so that he can preserve his nest-egg in addition to his rather small pension, for a combined total of 45,000 baht in spending per month. He doesn't need to save any money, so these figures should be right. Jim lives in a small attached home and pays for it to be cleaned once per week out of the miscellaneous category. Out of the same category he can get a proper barber experience once per week which includes a shave (200 baht for haircut and a shave!). Jim has health insurance and goes to a great gym club where he can use the saunas and pool. He loves taking his motorbike to the beach and he even takes care of his cat. He eats a great Thai diet and goes to good local Thai restaurants and gets some local beers with his buddies once or twice per week. He can also take complete care of his live-in girlfriend, but he can't afford to send her family any money since he is on a fixed-income budget. Even with the girlfriend who does his laundry and goes to dinner with him, Jim squeezes in a weekly naughty massage and even sees a bar girl twice a month.

Jim has a pretty darn good life since he isn't working. His lifestyle does require discipline since there is not enough room for Jim to do something stupid like start drinking a lot or get hustled by a bar girl. He makes it home once per year, but he doesn't have extra money to go traveling in Thailand unless he takes a bus, stays in a bungalow, and doesn't see any bar girls or massage girls that month. Jim has an annual retirement visa fee of close to 20,000 baht (including lawyer) so he takes things easy in the month it's due, and doesn't get much "entertainment" for a few weeks to offset the expense. Aside from the tight line he has to walk with his budget, Jim's biggest problem will be if he is healthy enough to stay on the planet for a long time, since he isn't prepared for inflation. In twenty years Jim's lifestyle will be shot with his spending power at 45,000 baht. Even good ol' Bob is better prepared for inflation because at least his salary is likely to rise in proportion. But if Jim wants to keep up the lifestyle for decades, he'd probably have to take on a teaching job at some point.

Robert, a 60-year-old man who was never rich but always saved and owned property. After liquidating his entire assets, Robert comes to Thailand with 15,000,000 baht and some type of pension that brings in 30,000 baht per month.

Rent	30,000 baht per month
Electric	2,000 baht per month
Bank fees	900 baht per month
Phone	300 baht per month
Internet	900 baht per month
Food	6,000 baht per month
Miscellaneous	7,300 baht per month
Entertainment	30,000 baht per month
Visit-home fund	5,000 baht per month
Vacation fund	5,000 baht per month
Health related	4,500 baht per month
Gym club	600 baht per month
Total	92,500 baht per month

What's crazy is that by many Western standards, Robert doesn't have enough to retire, with $500,000 USD or 357,000 euro. This would be considered enough to barely squeeze out a retirement in many cities, but in Thailand, Robert will be living an awesome life! I'm figuring that spending 5 per cent of his nest egg per year, plus his pension, will add up to 92,500 baht per month. He'll have a modern and spacious home with a pool and it will be cleaned regularly. He can visit his home country once per year in style or he can go twice if he really wants to. He can also take nice little weekend-trips to beautiful places in Thailand. He doesn't have to worry about health costs and he eats a great diet and goes out whenever he feels like it. Robert has enough money in his entertainment fund to have a girlfriend and see more girls on the side than he'll know what to do with, as long as he follows the rules set forth in this book. He can do just about any activities and take on any hobbies that he chooses. As inflation rises he might have to make some sacrifices, but after 20 years he may be willing to slowly dip into his nest-egg to offset these sacrifices.

William, a 45-year-old man who is bringing 20,000,000 baht to Thailand after liquidating his assets which came as a result of some inheritance, some savings, and some real estate. William doesn't have a pension but he plans to keep busy by working as a teacher with a 45,000 baht salary. An educated man and a good writer, William also freelances online and makes 25,000 baht per month from that, and those incomes are "after tax" (taxes would be minimal anyway).

Rent	30,000 baht per month
Electric	2,500 baht per month
Bank fees	900 baht per month
Phone	300 baht per month
Internet	1,200 baht per month
Food	8,000 baht per month
Miscellaneous	10,000 baht per month
Entertainment	40,000 baht per month
Visit-home fund	20,000 baht per month
Vacation fund	20,000 baht per month
Health related	3,000 baht per month
Gym club	600 baht per month
Total	136,500 baht per month

William could afford not to work, but he's in the peak working years of his life so that would be silly. The extra money adds to his luxury. I calculated William only spending 4 per cent of his nest egg per year. Considering that he can afford to be slightly more aggressive with his investment portfolio than the older guys, spending only 4 per cent of his assets each year should offset any inflation over time. You'll notice that his "vacation fund" and his "visit home fund" are very high. I am figuring that William has two children in their early twenties. William wants to visit his children often and he likes to explore Thailand's most beautiful beaches and islands frequently. William lives in a great house and it's always cleaned and he doesn't even have to cook. He can do just about anything he wants to every night. He works, so instead of seeing a bar girl twenty times per month, which he can easily do, he chooses instead to see some high-end Gogo superstars several times per month on weekends, and mixes in a full-time girlfriend and the occasional naughty massage and bar girl. He has the sex-life of a Greek God! He also eats like a champion and can do any hobby or activity he pleases. Let's face it, William is living the dream in Thailand.

An exact budget will depend on your personal situation, your habits, the city you pick etc. You can use the above examples as an average guide. 30,000 baht is the minimum amount you'll want to be able to spend every month, and you always have to have a plan for the future which includes retirement and/or inflation. With only 30,000 baht to spend a month, you should have a few million baht savings that is at least earning compound interest for you. Again 30,000 baht is by no means a great luxurious lifestyle. It's getting by decently in Thailand in some version of a very simple lifestyle. I think some 50 per cent of people would find living in their home country to be a better alternative.

If you are a disciplined person who has no problems with temptation, 45,000-baht-spending per month would probably provide a better lifestyle than most single men have in your home country. For that money you still have no real luxury, but you have no worries. You have a decent-enough place to live, you eat well, you can do a lot of activities, and you can have a good sex-life and/or a girlfriend. In a beautiful place with a great climate and lots of beautiful women, your quality of life should be good.

Being able to spend 60,000 baht a month in Thailand is a real benchmark for a high quality of life. If you can manage to spend that without any problems, you are sure to live better than almost anyone in your home country. People making five times as much in your home country would probably still be envious of your lifestyle.

At 75,000+, forget it. It's being pampered by women every day and having everything taken care of for you. There are of course many men who spend this amount and don't live a great lifestyle, but they haven't read my book and probably spend most of it on their bar-girl wife and her family. Using everything you learn in the book, you can live like a king for 75,000 and up in Thailand.

There are some wealthy people out there and I haven't really written any chapters with them in mind. But surely there are people who can spend 200,000 baht per month in Thailand without flinching and without ever worrying about retirement or inflation. If you're in that group you'd be crazy not to come to Thailand. You'd be living in a beautiful house with an amazing pool and you'd always have a couple of the hottest girls around with you at all times. You'd be going to the most exotic islands and the best restaurants whenever you wanted. You'd have a cook and a housekeeper and transportation provided wherever and whenever you wanted to go.

Motorbikes vs. cars

Cars are expensive in Thailand; the taxes on importing cars are through the roof and they just don't depreciate as they should. I have seen basic prices at near double the cost of prices in the U.S. And if you ship a car from your home country you'll pay a hefty tax. Insurance companies can't be trusted here, and I've heard of some people whose insurance denied them, without good reason, on claims that should have been covered. Parking in many cities is a big problem, and driving a car on some small roads filled with food vendors, crazy motorbike drivers, dogs, and plenty of foot-traffic is a stressful endeavor. For these reasons I don't recommend buying a car unless you really have the funds available and you just use it for long-distance drives, which is when it would actually help.

New motorbikes are cheap, usually around 45,000 baht for a good one, and you can get one cheap at an auction if you put some time into it. Motorbikes are dangerous, and most people who drive them long enough run into some type of accident. Whether that accident is minor or major may not be under your control, but knowing that the odds are that you'll eventually have an issue is scary, to say the least. Motorbikes happen to be the best option for many short destination errands, and I think it's essential to learn how to drive one at some point. You don't have to be in any type of rush, and you should have someone who is very experienced hop on the back and teach you for hours and hours as you go from easy roads to more difficult roads. Don't even try to drive a motorbike in Bangkok unless you have many months' worth of experience. It's not just about knowing how to drive the bike; it's about knowing how to drive the bike in Thailand. In any case, the best advice is to only drive the motorbike when you have to, and never if you have alcohol in your system. Limiting the amount you use the bike will limit the chances of something going wrong. You can be the best driver in the world, but if a Thai driver isn't looking because "they're leaving it up to Buddha," you're not very well-protected on one of those things if someone hits you. New motorbikes get stolen all of the time in Thailand, and usually they're only half-way covered, if that, in terms of the "guarantee". Make sure you have a good locking mechanism and make sure you always use it. They get stolen from busy shopping malls in broad daylight, so there is no situation where you can say, "I'll be back soon enough." Don't drive on the Songkran water-festival holiday. People will pelt you with water as you're driving, and unfortunately many people die each year because of this.

Bottom line: Don't have a car unless you're wealthy. You'll need a motorbike, but driving one is risky, so limit the time you use it. Never drive drunk and never trust other drivers in Thailand; drive as defensively as possible.

Staying in touch with friends and family

I've talked a bit about this in other sections and chapters. Basically, modern technology has made it easier and cheaper than ever to keep in touch. Skype video chat, Facebook, bulk-picture email attachment features, cellular instant messaging, and cheap Voip phone rates (like Skype has), make it very easy to keep a relationship going with your friends, and it makes it easy to document your adventures. I think it's best to visit home once per year, but not everyone's budget will allow for that. When you are visiting home it can be frantic, and you'll need to visit anyone who considers you a friend so as not to offend them. It can actually be a bit bizarre and confusing when you visit home, but it's a must as you can't afford to throw away your life-long friends and family members.

Don't lose your verbal skills

Staying in touch with your friends and family members and talking to them on the phone often will go a long way towards making sure that you don't lose some of your verbal skills. It happens to people here. They stop using English so much, and whenever they speak it's in broken English so their spouse or Thai friends can understand. When they do spend time with English-speaking people here it's usually in a bar setting so they're not exactly breaking out the big vocabulary guns. A few years of this can really take its toll. If you were forced to go back home and get a job, you may have an adjustment period to get back into the swing of things with your verbal abilities. The easiest way to make sure it doesn't happen is to talk to your friends and family on the phone often.

Hopefully you have a friend or two that you have intellectual conversations with; make the most of the opportunities with them.

Gym

Living in Thailand makes it easy to get into the best shape of your life. Here you're likely to have cheap gym memberships, ample free time, and no weather excuses. Personal training sessions are cheaper here than in almost any other place in the world, and there are some good gyms and trainers around. I suggest joining a club where you have pools, saunas, and hot tubs available. Twenty-four hour places that have these amenities are a blessing. Thailand gym clubs are cheap,

especially for the one-year rates. Some gyms offer "forever packages," but I suggest only doing one year. This is because expats are known to move home, or at least to a new city pretty often, and I have heard some bad stories of people who bought a lifetime membership only to be told a year later that it's no good. If that happens to you there's nothing you can do about it, so it's not worth the risk.

Phone, internet, cable, sporting events

Up until very recently, Thailand's communication methods were light-years behind, and this was actually a significant downside to many who lived here. It's in a lot better shape now, and I don't see it as being a problem at all anymore.

Phone

I talked a lot about this in the money-saving tips, but I'll go over it again. You want to make sure you get a Skype account going in your home country with a subscription to talk unlimited to people from home. Do not leave this until you get to Thailand, because you will not be able to purchase the subscription with an account started anywhere in Asia. Once you have a subscription you can purchase a phone number that will come up on caller ID and that people can call you on. Buy the subscription first and you can get the number at half price. It costs me less than 2,000 baht per year for the Skype account, the U.S. phone number, and the unlimited subscription. Thanks to the Skype mobile application, I can call out and receive calls even when I'm not at home.

You'll need to get your smart phone unlocked if it isn't already. You can have this done almost anywhere. To really make things affordable, prepay sim cards to talk to people within Thailand, and prepay an internet data plan for your cellular as well. Make sure you know how to turn the internet on and off completely on your phone (including GPS and email), and then use the data minutes only as you need them. Most new cell phones have wifi, so when you're in your house you never need to pay for your data. It'll cost around 200 baht for fifty hours of data, and as long as you're good about turning it off when you're not using it, that should be more than enough. The system is almost too good to be true, so let's hope it doesn't change anytime soon. Also you should know that 4g probably won't be in Thailand for at least five years, and 3g is rolling out very slowly as we speak and won't be nationwide until 2012. Many good smart phones can tether an internet connection for free once they're unlocked. This means that your cell phone becomes a wifi hotspot, and your laptop or tablet can pick up the connection easily. This helps if you're traveling in Thailand because some good hotels don't even have internet or charge too much to use it, and it's usually slow. The tethered connection isn't fast since its 2g, and when its 3g it'll make mobile internet computing that much easier. When 4g hits Thailand, you really won't need to pay for home internet because your phone will be fast enough to give you DSL speeds on your computer. Again, we're years and years away from 4g as it stands now.

Internet

If you're far from a major city and in the middle of nowhere you could face an uphill battle to get a good internet connection, but this is still true in many quiet areas of first-world countries. As long as you're in or very near a city that people have heard of, you'll be able to find something pretty good these days. It used to be a huge problem to get a good connection, but Thailand is catching up. If you're in a house and the internet is important to you, you'll want to find something very solid. They'll give you the option of paying for it monthly or getting a huge discount if you prepay six months or one year. You can find reliable 10Mbps download speeds for about $250 per six months. If you don't download and stream television, then you can get something good enough for about $250 per year. Some apartment buildings in Thailand charge you for internet and they abuse you because they don't have enough power to properly serve the amount of residents in the building, which results in very poor speeds. One of the buildings I was in let me buy my own private connection, but I was on the second floor and I'm not sure how viable it would have been if I'd been on the twentieth floor. Either way you should look into getting a dedicated internet connection because most apartment buildings charge you a lot for inferior service. The internet is important enough for some to let it impact their decision on picking a place to live in. If it's this way for you, double-check to make sure the internet situation is to your liking. This could be another advantage to living in a house, unless you're lucky enough to find a building that gives you proper internet speeds at a fair price, which is rare.

Cable

In Chapter 8, under the section "Watch TV for free", I give you some good tips for watching everything you want to for free, or close to it, using an internet connection and easily connecting your TV to your computer. Basic cable is cheap; it might even be free depending on where you live. In a house, basic cable would cost you about 4,000 baht per year. The basic cable comes with a few British or American news channels, a few movie channels in English, a couple of sports channels that only play soccer and occasionally rugby, the sci-fi channel, and the universal channel which plays "Law and Order" about twelve times a day. This is good enough for me to get by since I download or steam everything else I want to watch. Actually I don't miss anything this way, and have just enough channels to watch something interesting when I don't have anything downloaded or cued to stream. You can also pay 2,000 baht or more per month for an actual cable box, and upgrade to have a Tivo if you insist. You get some more channels this way, but it's still not like being at home, and I think it's a waste of money.

Sporting events

The big soccer events are always on at bars and even some restaurants.   Some of them are on basic cable for free and all of them can be watched with the right package and a real cable box and cable provider. U.S. sports are harder to come by.   There is an American sports package that plays some of the NFL games, some hockey, baseball, and UFC events. Since the games are on at very odd Thailand times, it's difficult to find bars with

American sporting events, but they're out there. In the big cities, you can always catch the Monday Night football game Tuesday morning at an Irish Pub, and you'll have no issues finding UFC fights or the Super Bowl. It's strange to watch the Super Bowl in the morning, but there are enough real NFL fans here to enjoy it.

Shopping tips

It shouldn't be difficult to track down some good deals no matter what you're buying, with the exception of cars and electronics of course. Try to bring in your smaller electronics from your home country and wait for sales if you're buying something like a TV or a computer. Big C and similar big-box shops such as Tesco and Lotus are cheap, but they're not cheap enough on some items. In Big C I only purchase items that I need that most Thai people don't consider a "need" and which therefore aren't stocked in Thai markets. Big C might also be the cheapest on imported alcohol, so it comes in handy for that. It also comes in handy as a one-stop shop if you have many things to buy and don't feel like going all over the city. Otherwise, Thai markets will wipe the floor with Big C on many items.

Clothing from a Thai market or "flea market" is very affordable, especially if you or your Thai friend is negotiating to get "The Real Thai Price." If you need to buy a lot of clothing, like a wardrobe's worth, you might check out Bobai Market or Chatuchak in Bangkok where you'll find anything you need for very cheap. There are a lot of people at these markets so make sure you're careful with your wallet.

7-11 and Family Mart shops are actually not expensive, and if you can walk to one, it might save money to use them for a few items compared to paying for transportation to get to big box stores. There are many furniture shops that look like warehouses but sell retail and maybe a little wholesale. They might be making the furniture in the back which is fine. They're very cheap and if you twist their arm they'll deliver your furniture for free. As with anything else, just make sure you have a Thai friend negotiating for you like it's their purchase.

Cell Phones are expensive in Thailand. People used to fund their vacations by selling a lot of hard-to-get phones in Thailand while they were here. It's not so easy to do that anymore, but the prices are still too high if you're buying here. Just avoid buying a good phone here; I think that's the best bet. This is one of the only items that makes sense to have your friend buy and ship it to you.

Buying jewelry in Thailand isn't recommended either. Gold tends to be expensive, and gems may be fake or partially fake. If you're looking for nice things to buy your girlfriend, nice flowers are cheap and easy to find and she'll enjoy buying a bag-full of clothing at a Thai market. If you have to buy her something a little nicer, consider getting her a cell phone off of Craigslist when you're visiting home. I got an I-phone 3gs from someone I met on Craigslist in the U.S. for 4,700 baht. You can't get it cheaper than 15,000 in Thailand (even though the I-phone 5 is coming out soon). So when I gave it to my girlfriend as a present she said it was the nicest present anyone had ever given her in her entire life and she literally cried with happiness. Also if you have to get jewelry, go with your girlfriend and let her pick out gold in a Thai Jewelry store and not at a modern-looking Western shopping mall where you'll get murdered. Thai women like the type of gold necklaces and bracelets that have been out of style in the West for more than thirty years. This is what they like, and who are we to try and get them to change? Expect to spend about 10,000 baht for a gold necklace they will love. You can usually get these shops down by about 10 per cent on their prices if you have the baht with you in your hand.

I know in the U.S. there are many "Dollar Stores" that can be quite reasonable on many small necessity items. I have seen similar shops in Thailand where everything is 20 baht and in some weekly traveling carnivals I have seen them set up 10 baht shops. All I can say is that they're amazing! You can load up on little things you need for your home. You can spend 300 baht and you'd have a hard time carrying everything home with you.

Food

For food shopping, some of the Super Markets have good prices on meat and vegetables, similar to Thai market prices, but they're very high on any Western brands. It's best to eat "made in Thailand" brands and to train yourself to eat a lot of meat and vegetables. The Thai markets are cheap and the vegetables and fruit are wonderful. I actually don't buy fruit in the supermarkets because nothing beats the fruit from the fruit vendors. Mangosteen and Rambutan are two fruits common only to Southeast Asia and are abundant and cheap in Thailand. They're also considered the next exotic, breakthrough, cancer-fighting fruits by some Western Scientists, nutritionists, and doctors; health nuts back home are paying ten times what you have to pay you get your fix. By the way, they're both delicious.

In regard to meats, I recommend going to the supermarkets until you have fully adjusted to Thai food. The outdoor meat vendors at the Thai markets don't have temperature-controlled refrigerators for the bulk of their meat and it just sits outside in the hot sun. The selection on soft drinks isn't good, and Thai people evidently like double or even triple the sugar per serving in a soft drink, making them undrinkable for many of us. It's hot outside, so try to stick to water.

Thai restaurants use too much salt and MSG. The MSG is toxic but Thais just don't seem to care. Make sure to say, "Mai sai phong churot" so they know not to give you MSG. I have come to accept that there's going to be too much salt in my restaurant food, and I'd rather have the salt than the MSG. The food sold by street vendors and even some small restaurants is so cheap that cooking your own food can actually cost you slightly more sometimes. It's a matter of health, and if you're a health-conscious person you'll make sure to eat meat and vegetables from a supermarket consistently throughout a given week without the crazy amounts of salt and with zero MSG.

This isn't a health-food book, but I'll point out what I have seen in my experience. If you eat like most Thais, you'll eat a lot of meats, vegetables, and fruit and of course rice. This is likely to be a significant improvement from your Western diet, so you'll lose weight and be relatively healthy. If you can cut out the rice and the noodles and just stick with water, meat, vegetables, and fruit you will be in fantastic shape before long. I find that this kind of diet is almost impossible to stick to in the U.S., but it's really easy in Thailand. You just eat like them, minus the rice and noodles (and the MSG of course).

Making new friends

It's easy enough to meet people in a place where everyone is looking to have a good time. Certainly retirees will find no shortage of people to meet at any of the local bars. Younger folks can make friends with some of the locals, and should also find friends from their home country and in their age group in any of the cities. Younger people tend to leave more often, so it's possible that you'll make a lot of friends with people who are just there on vacation, but there's nothing wrong with that. If you have a steady stream of your old friends visiting you, and one or two Thailand vacationers you occasionally meet, you'll always be meeting someone coming into town. And you're sure to meet a few folks with similar interest who live here permanently. Bars and the gym are typically the best places to make friends. There are some ex-pat clubs as well, but I believe they are more for retirees. You can Google these clubs for more information; I understand that some of them got shut down because they had no permits. I think the best clubs are in Bangkok. Also, social networking sites like Facebook make it easy to meet other expats.

Health Care

In talking to many people about health care, the most common reaction I get is that it's great and affordable near all of the cities, but if you're in the middle of nowhere you could be in trouble. Having actual health insurance is very cheap and it's a recommended option for those who have children or those who are over 45. If you're younger and you're healthy, I don't think it's necessary to pay for health insurance because hospital, doctor, and medication fees are as low as it gets on the chance that you'd even need them.

The dentists in the cities are so cheap and so good that I would recommend anyone who needs some dental work to get it done while here on vacation. The only downside is that they don't offer nitrous oxide, but novocain gets the job done if you're getting something bitchy done.

Chapter 10: 50 THINGS TO DO IN THAILAND BESIDES THE OBVIOUS

1) Take up Meditation. We're not talking about a religious activity at all. All studies show that mediation has a positive impact on your body.

2) Learn Muay Thai kickboxing and let a former professional train you. It's the national sport of Thailand and it's a great way to get in shape. It's also a lot of fun and a real challenge to your mind and body.

3) Wind surfing is a great and cheap sport to pick up here. You should pay a professional to teach you all of the safety procedures, and its best to never go deep into the Ocean alone.

4) Excellent gyms are affordable and there are good trainers available for cheap as well.

5) Hiking in certain areas of Thailand can be a truly amazing experience. Take a guide with you and bring water and your camera.

6) Kayaking is great exercise and it's not a risky sport unless you're going deep into the ocean, which you should not do. You should also only go when waters are calm, and lakes are the best bet.

7) Thailand also makes the perfect backdrop in many cities for mountain biking. Make sure you're never in any busy roads, and don't go at night.

8) You can learn how to give a Thai massage here with a few-hour class for cheap enough. Future women in your life won't be able to resist your magic hands once you pick up the techniques.

9) Golfing in a beautiful location doesn't get much cheaper than in Thailand. Golf pros will give you lessons for well below the going rate in your home country as well.

10) Become an expert marksman at any of the shooting ranges available in every major city in Thailand.

11) Go on an elephant trek and make sure it goes through water; it's a crazy experience when the elephant is taking you through fairly deep waters that are no match for them.

12) Learn how to cook Thai food like a professional at a Thai cooking school. Like most activities in Thailand, it won't run you a huge bill and you'll learn to cook some meals that will impress any woman.

13) Visit the neighboring countries of Viet Nam, Laos, and Cambodia. Each has its own niche and traveling from Thailand is more than affordable. Don't forget your passport and make sure you have re-entry permission on your visa.

14) Parasailing isn't really a sport, but for 800 baht in most places you can have quite a fifteen-minute adventure.

15) The scuba diving in Thailand is top notch and perhaps the best in the world when you factor in price. You can get certified here and you'll be on your way.

16) If diving is too extreme for you, snorkeling is a good backup.

17) Jungle tours are a blast and there is a popular one that has tree-top zip lines scattered throughout the tour.

18) There are some cave tours in Thailand that are like nothing you have ever seen before.

19) There are some white-water rafting trails in if you're looking for adventure.

20) ATV courses are popular all over Thailand as well, and you'll find the prices to be more than worth the experience.

21) How can you beat a one-hour long full-body oil massage by an expert Thai masseuse for 300 baht?

22) Visit some temples that are hundreds of years old. Cambodia is the best of the breed for this, but Thailand is no slouch.

23) Plastic surgery is cheap in Thailand and you can find a reputable doctor if you take the search for one seriously. Hair transplants at 75 per cent off the cost, anyone?

24) Internationally known for its Tattoo availability and prices, if this is your type of thing, get some ink done right after washing a cold Singha beer down.

25) The movie theatres in Thailand kick ass. The seats are comfortable, the prices are great, and most major films come out with Thai subtitles so your girlfriend can enjoy it too.

26) Rent a bungalow on a desolate beach and have a honeymoon type of weekend for next to nothing. There are many beautiful beaches that aren't popular with tourists (not in Phuket and Koh Samuit) where you can do this.

27) Are you an adrenaline junky? Sky-diving and bungee-jumping are available from north to south in Thailand; just do a little internet research to make sure you're going with a safe company that has a perfect record.

28) Want to see something you can't see at home? Ping Pong and other sex shows are available, and thankfully without any donkeys.

29) Check out a Floating Market where vendors on small boats sell all types of food and other goods.

30) See amazing waterfalls. There are some that are second-to-none in Thailand.

31) Visit a Northern Hill Tribe. If you want to see what Thailand was like 500 years ago, check a tribe out for a day and you'll be very intrigued.

32) Rock climbing and mountain hiking are popular in certain parts of Thailand. Use a guide and don't take on more than you should.

33) Go to an exotic island, like Krabi, and see the most beautiful waters in the world.

34) You'll find no shortage of local catch if you like to fish.

35) Camping tours and equipment are available.

36) Go sailing or learn how to sail.

37) Hire a long-tail boat on an exotic island.

38) Walk on a beautiful beach.

39) Enjoy five-star quality meals at restaurants that are very inexpensive.

40) Go to the Full Moon party on Koh Phang-Ngan.

41) Rent a motorcycle and go cruising.

42) Float down The River Kwai.

43) Go shopping with unbelievable prices on clothing and souvenirs.

44) Get a portrait painting done by a high-level professional at a fraction of the cost back home.

45) Paintball with a few friends.

46) Go on a speed-boat tour.

47) Bird-watch to find some exotic bird species.

48) Explore your photography hobby with unlimited photo opportunities.

49) See a live show or band. Whether it's in Thai or you're seeing a cover band, you'll be entertained.

50) Eat on a boat-restaurant or dinner-cruise.

Chapter 11: OPENING A BUSINESS IN THAILAND

Many retirees or young entrepreneurs come to Thailand with thoughts of opening a small bar or scuba shop where they'll "live the life". Nearly all get their asses handed to them, and it's as simple as that. It's a system that is set up for total failure, and the few who miraculously find a way to make it work would have been ten times more successful doing so elsewhere. So if you're coming to Thailand, don't come here thinking you'll find a nice side-business income while you're here, even if you're the type that has always done so at home. And if you haven't had a lot of business experience in your country then I advise you to not even consider it here. You may find ways to run businesses in your home country online while you live in Thailand, but that is a whole other animal. And of course large and well-funded businesses can expand here and bypass many of the common problems. But we're talking about opening a small Thai business in Thailand and expecting to make money, which just doesn't happen often.

Why it does not work

If you make good money in Thailand, you are set up for a great life and everyone knows this. So if you try and buy an existing business, such as an "established bar," you have to ask yourself why anyone would sell a profitable business in Thailand. Buying businesses in Thailand almost never works out well. Even if it was profitable, it likely depended a great deal on the personal relationships the owner and the manager had with its customers. Those customers will not just give you the benefit of the doubt, and so any past performance is not even close to being indicative of future results. And the documents you see for past revenues and/or "profit and loss statements" can't be trusted. If someone sells you their business and it turns out that everything they told you was a complete lie, what are you going to do about it? You don't have the benefit of a fair system like you might at home, and if anything goes wrong you're really limited in your options. Also, lawyers will be licking their chops over trying to broker a business-sale and it's very common that they overcharge and don't deliver.

"Ok, I won't buy a business; I'll just start one from scratch." If only it were that easy. First, you can only own 49 per cent of a business here. Seriously, you're not even allowed to own 50 per cent of a business that you will put all of the funds and work into. I should be able to stop right there as going any further will be overkill. Why in the world would you want to go into business if you can't even own it? But there are lines of men eager to put 51 per cent of their businesses into their Thai girlfriends' names so I'll continue to further educate you on the numerous other pitfalls. But in case you didn't draw the conclusion by now, you can't stop your Thai partner from taking the business from you. You may be in love or you may think she's in love with you, but that doesn't actually matter. Any relationship can sour, and when it does, there goes your business. Knowing that she owns the business, she might not exactly be scared of the relationship ending, and it may even motivate her to end it. This really doesn't even matter unless the business is at least somewhat successful, which it probably won't be. But to know that, even if you surpass all obstacles and make a nice business, it can be stolen out from under you and you can't do much to stop it... that should make an impact on you.

The business visa and the work permit associated with it is also tricky, and although it's hard to actually get a grasp on how to properly do this, we know that it involves mountains of paper work, government fees, legal fees, accounting fees, and a decent amount of money held up in a Thai bank account (perhaps 3 million baht) which probably won't be earning you interest. It's a nasty process, and if you are operating illegally then you open yourself up to deportation, fines, blacklisting, and in the worst case a short stint in a Thai prison that's sure to change your life.

If that's not enough to stop you, please understand the general attitude amongst the Thai people and the Thai police. They want you to come here and spend money; they do not want you to come here and make money. They don't see it as though you will be creating jobs; they see it as though you will be hurting Thai business owners that you will compete with. This means at times you'll face issues with Thai police and Thai mafia that just give you "fines" or "regulation fees." It doesn't matter how you look at it, these will come, and if you don't pay then you are risking your livelihood. If you do pay, then they know they can keep coming back. You really need to make an alliance with someone (police, army, Thai mafia, Russian mafia) to protect you from other soliciting groups, and this alliance will come with a monthly fee. Also, if you have a lease on your space with a Thai landlord, don't expect the law to go to bat for you if the Thai breaks the lease and either tells you to leave or doubles your rent at the first sign of you actually doing well. The law will always favor the Thai citizen, and who knows what unethical things might be done outside of court if you are actually fighting a matter inside of court.

You may have deep pockets and you may be able to square a lot of these issues with the best lawyers in town. I think you're better off keeping that money or risking it in a better business climate, but let's assume that you're willing to spare no expense in terms of making it possible. What kind of business would you start here that would work and have the profit potential to warrant a large investment? Exporting used to be an easy way to take advantage of your two-country base. You would find some businesses in your home country and offer them inventory and supplies at a deep discount at Asia prices. Unfortunately China now owns this type of market, and sites like Alibaba.com make it easy for any retailer or wholesaler in the West to meet English-speaking employees at Chinese factories. Your business in Thailand can't compete with the Chinese factories. What about restaurants and hotels? The competition will be considerable and the off-season months will be a killer. The disadvantages you face compared to the Thai businessman are great and overwhelming to say the least.

I do need to make it clear that there are some small-business men who have succeed legally in Thailand, and possibly even in the bar/Gogo/restaurant type of industries. In almost every case, the men were well-connected in Thailand and had significant business experience in the restaurant, bar, or strip-club scene in their country. For every one of these success stories there are probably fifty people who seemed to know what they were doing and failed. Still, extremely well-connected, funded and experienced business players have made it work here and I'm sure more will come. I guess what I would take out of that is that doing business in Thailand may eventually become possible if you make the right connections and friends over the course of years, and learn every trick in the book so you don't have to learn the hard way.

The bottom line: this is not a good place to open a business, and if you don't want to take my word for it do some "Googling" to read about the million-and-one horror stories. Also keep in mind that shame and embarrassment prevent most from admitting their mistakes here. Many bar owners are just happy not to lose money with their business, and that's actually pretty difficult to pull off!

Is there any way to bring in some extra income?

As I stated before, you can find ways to make money online from your home country and pay taxes on it in your home country. This isn't easy either and there are a lot of scams out there. The working model for it is if you're a skilled writer or web/graphic designer. Then you can use sites such as **elance.com** and **freelancer.com** to bring in some income. You probably won't get rich doing this but if you're skilled you can make extra money.

The other interesting option is available to anyone that has a long-term girlfriend or wife. You want to avoid starting a business with them, but you can let them have a small business. So let's say your Thai wife or girlfriend has some experience selling clothing, doing hair/nails, or cooking staple Thai dishes. There is nothing stopping you from giving her the money to open the business as a gift. If she has experience it wouldn't be uncommon for her to open a small shop, salon, or a little food shop for very little money (maybe 60,000 to 75,000 baht) and to bring in some extra money each month, perhaps 15,000 to 20,000 baht profit per month if she's good. It's a low-risk, low-reward type of situation. If she doesn't have a work ethic then you'll just waste the money, but as long as you trust her work ethic and she has experience, the numbers I mentioned above are reasonable. It also wouldn't be out of the question for her to expand, possibly opening a new location and doubling her profit. I think anything more than that would be problematic. Now you don't own even 1 per cent of the business so if you guys split up, obviously you're not getting your investment back. But for as long as you are together and on good standing, if she's willing to take the money she earns and contribute it towards your combined expenses, then you may have a nice little situation. It would be as if she had a decent job, but with more flexibility, I suppose. At the very least a small working business she owns will get you off the hook for having to send her family anything.

info@thaigirlspattayagirls.com

Chapter 12: BASIC THAI WORDS AND PHRASES

Thai isn't as difficult to learn as many other Asian languages are, and lea
won't be a huge undertaking. A nice way to learn is to have your lady friends teacn you
words and phrases each day. You can keep a log of each word or phrase you learn in your phone
and read them over whenever you're bored. By doing this you'll pick things up quickly and you'll get
the tones down well. which is hard when teaching yourself out of a book. There are slightly
different dialects of Thai which complicate things, but basic Thai will work nation-wide. Here is a list
of what I would consider "the basics." It's best to go through the words with a Thai lady since the
pronunciations are a bit up to interpretation, especially when you try and convert them into English.

GREETINGS

Hello = Sawa dee
Thank you (man says) = Kob Khun Krap
Thank you (woman says) = Kob Khun Ka
How are you? = Khun sabai di mai?
I am fine thanks (man says) = Pom sabai di krap
I am fine thanks (woman says) =Chan sabai di ka

*Basically women say "ka" at the end of a sentence
while men say "krap".*

You're welcome = Yin dee krap / ka
Wait = Roh sakru
I (man) = pom
I (woman) = chan
Come = ma
Come from = ma jak
I come from Australia = Pom ma jak pratet Australia (man)
= Chan ma jak pratet Australia (woman)
Go = pai
Gone already = pai leu
Go where = pai nai
Go soon = pai diauni

EATING

Eat = gin
Drink = deun
Food = ahan
Candies = kanom
Have you eaten already? = gin leu mai krap/ka?
Rice = kao
to eat = kin kao (literally: eat rice)
I am hungry = pom/chan heeu kao

hungry? = Khun heeu kao mai?

= aroy

ave eaten already thanks = Pom/chan kin leu krap/ka

I am full thank you = Pom/chan im leu krap/ka

Are you hungry? = khun heeu kao mai?

GENERAL

water	= nam
hard	= keng
ice	= nam keng (*hard water*)
hot water	= nam ron
cold water	= nam yen
waterfall	= nam toc
rain	= fon
raining	= fon toc
shower	= ab nam
maybe /perhaps	= Bang ti
play	= len
speak	= pud
funny	= sanuk
everything	= took sing
large	= yai
small	= lek
fast	= reu
slow	= cha
have	= mi
I have	= pom/chan mi
I don't have	= pom/chan mai mi
you have	= khun mi
you don't have	= khun mai mi
can not hear you	= mai dai yin khun
I can hear you	= pom/chan dai yin khun
work	= tam ngan
I want	= *this can be said many ways*: pom/chan ao; pom/chan tong karn; pom/ chan yak
I think	= pom kid wa
why	= tam mai
smells bad	= min
good	= di
very good	= di mak
bad	= mai di
weather	= akas
hot weather	= akas ron
cold wind	= lom yen
strong wind	= lom reng
bathroom / toilet	= hong nam

info@thaigirlspattayagirls.com

shower	= ab nam
to look	= du
to see	= hen
again	= ik krang
where is	= yu nai
over there	= ti nun
here	= ti ni
what	= arai
when	= meua arai
friend	= peuang
good friend	= peuang di
problem	= pang ha
room	= hong
water	= nam
toilet	= hong nam
Where is the toilet?	= hong nam yu nai?
to enter	= kao
to understand	= kao jai (literally: to enter the heart)
don't understand	= mai kao jai

FEELINGS

good	= di
broken	= sia
heart	= jai
happy	= di jai (literally good heart)
afraid	= klua
hurt/pain	= jeb
never mind	= mai pen rai
frightened/scared	= pom/chan klua
Are you happy ?	= khun di jai mai?
I am sick	= pom/ chan mai sabai
I am happy	= pom/chan mi cuam suk; or pom chan sabai di
I am not happy	= pom/ chan mai sabai di
I am sad	= pom/ chan sia jai (literally I have a broken heart)
I am sorry	= pom/ chan koh tot
I am confused	= pom/chan sap son
I forget	= Pom/ chan leum leu
I have a problem	= pom/chan mi pang ha

CONVERSATIONS

I know	= pom/chan ru
I dont know	= pom/ chan mai ru
want	= ao
don't want	= mai ao

now	= ton ni
today	= wan ni
tonight	= keun ni
this morning	= chao ni
tomorrow	= prung ni
yesterday	= Meua wan
hour	= mong
What time is it?	= Ton ni gi mong?
Do you have a boyfriend ?	= khun mi fen leu mai?
I don't understand	= mai kao jai (literally: "doesn't enter the heart")
no thanks	= mai ao krap/ka
I don't know	= mai ru krap/ka
I don't like it	= mai chob krap/ka
pretty	= na rak (literally lovely face)
beautiful	= sway
handsome	= loh
breasts	= nom
kiss	= jup
like	= chob
You are very beautiful	= khun sway mak
You are very pretty	= khun na rak mak
to love	= rak
What is your name?	= khun cheu arai?
You have a beautiful smile	= khun mi yim sway
Happy to meet you	= pom mi cuam suk ti dai pop khun
See you again	= leu pop khun
Do you have a boy friend?	= khun mi fen leu mai?
I like you	= pom/chan chob khun
What are you thinking?	= khun kid arai?
I am shy	= pom ki ai
You look good	= khun sway di
You look beautiful	= khun sway mak
I will love you a long time	= pom/chan rak khun nan leu
Come watch a movie with me	= pai du nang kap pom/chan mai?
Come eat with me	= pai kin kao kap pom/chan mai?
to tell a lie	= pud go hok
shit	= ki
lies a lot	= pud ki mak (literally:" speaks shit a lot")
to promise	= hai sanya
sorry	= ko tot
to sleep	= non/ lap
to wake up	= teun
eyes	= ta
to close your eyes (go to sleep)	= lap ta
dreams	= fan; good night= lap fan di

I love Thailand	= Pom/chan rak Meuang Thai.
I love you	= pom/chan rak khun
I have come	= ma leu

INSULTS

stupid	= ting tong
pickle brain	= samong dong
dumb/ brainless	= mai mi samong
bad person	= jai dam (*literally: black heart*)
hot headed	= jai ron (*literally: hot heart*)
crazy	= ba
you are crazy	= khun ba
very/a lot	= mak
you are very crazy	= khun ba mak
stupid	= ting tong
you are stupid	= khun ting tong

NUMBERS:

1	= neung
2	= song
3	= sam
4	= si
5	= ha
6	= hok
7	= chet
8	= pet
9	= kao
10	= sip
11	= sip et
12	= sip song
13	= sip sam
14	= sip si
15	= sip ha
20	= yee sip
21	= yee sip et
22	= yee sip song
23	= yee sip sam
24	= yee sip si
25	= yee sip ha
30	= sam sip
40	= si sip
50	= ha sip
60	= hok sip
70	= chet sip
80	= pet sip

90	= kao sip
100	= neung roi
150	= neung roi ha sip
500	= ha roi
1000	= neung pan
1500	= neung pan ha roi
2000	= si pan
5000	= ha pan

TIME:

1 am = ti nung
2 am = ti song
3 am = ti sam
4 am = ti si
5 am = ti ha
6 am = hok mong chao
7 am = chet mong chao
8 am = pet mong chao
9 am = kao mong chao
10 am = sip mong chao
11 am = sip et mong
mid-day = tiang

1 pm = bai neung
2 pm = bai song
3 pm = bai sam
4 pm = si mong yen
5 pm = ha mong yen
6 pm = hok mong yen
7 pm = neung tum
8 pm = song tum
9 pm = sam tum
10 pm = si tum
11 pm = ha tum
midnight = tiang kheun

Chapter 13: CITY BY CITY GUIDE

There are hundreds of books written about some of the cities below. It's not for me to give you the history of each city and I can't even give you the names of places to go to since there is such a quick turnover and transition period for Gogo's, discos, and bars in Thailand. A recommended spot at the present time could be a complete disaster in just a few months. If you go to Chapter 17, you'll find a list of websites that keep an up to date log of which Gogo's, discos and bars you should go to. I use those websites, and they're good. What doesn't change are the basics in each city and how they compare to each other. So I will give you what you need to know and a little comparison of each of the major destinations in Thailand below. There are also plenty of great places to go in Thailand that are not listed below. Thailand is a decent-sized country and I can't mention every town and village in a country with a population of over 60,000,000 people.

I think it becomes fairly obvious which places will appeal to you the most. If you like "The Country" and you're budget-conscious, you might want to give Chiang Mai a look. If money isn't a problem, head down to Phuket and the nearby islands. Of course everyone should give Pattaya and Bangkok a look. The other places I mention are niche-vacation spots.

Pattaya

Pattaya is actually a decent-sized city. You won't find any office buildings but there are many hotels and high-rise apartment buildings. There is probably a higher percentage of prostitutes in Pattaya per 100 people than in any similarly sized or larger city in the world. New girls, old girls, Russian girls, pretty girls, drug-addict girls... you'll find all types in Pattaya. The main night-life center is called Walking Street, which is a long street ("soi") lined with nothing but lady bars, discos, and Gogos. Some of the streets that jut off of Walking Street, such as Soi Diamond, have legendary Gogos, and others are stacked with bars. You'll also find some pretty good food on Walking Street with views of the ocean. Walking Street is one of the most fun places to go to in the entire world for a guy who's looking. Prices aren't as cheap as they used to be, but you can find beer specials and you can always find a cute girl at a decent price. Stunners will cost more at the Gogos.

Soi 6

This is a "Pattaya-Only" adventure. Walking Street is its own entity as well, but that street ("soi") is lined with bars, Gogos and discos that all follow the rules of those establishment types described above. Soi 6 is unlike anything else though, and it's actually more of a daytime spot than anything else. It's a long block that connects to the main beach street in Pattaya. It is a one-of-a-kind place and everyone should see it for themselves. I once played a game with my friend in which we started walking at the beginning of the street to see who could make it the furthest without having a forty-five-minute detour. Neither of us made it very far. Actually if you frequent this street, you might want to start at the opposite end at times just to give the places at the other end a chance for your business.

Soi 6 is lined with bars, maybe thirty or so. Each place has girls outside trying to get your attention. Many of them will be hands-on with you and their aggressiveness towards you can be overwhelming in a good way, but in a slightly annoying way as well. It's ok to be picky, and if you're put on the spot, just say you are going to meet a friend and you might come back. Once you do find a girl who you like they'll take you into the bar where you can buy a round or two of drinks and talk. Then you'll negotiate terms, and she'll take you to a room upstairs for full service. You have to pay the house 300 for the room, and the girl will usually charge 700, although it's not uncommon for her to ask for more if she thinks she can get it. I usually just tell them I can give a total of 1,000 between her and the house and I've never been turned down or received any less than great service. I've also gone in for the two-girl splurge which was an extra 1,000. The bar tells you they charge for the room, but they're charging for the lady, so there's no 300 baht discount for two girls.

Soi 6 has many "new to the scene" girls which can add an exciting spice to the recipe.   Each bar is different, but it certainly seems as though some of the Mamasans in the Soi 6 bars are recruiting directly from Isan rather than from Pattaya. The Soi 6 gig is difficult for a girl because the hours start early in the day and there is little room for them to get a big payday from any one man, thanks to the in-and-out nature of the soi. Experienced girls who speak some English will quickly find themselves in a bar for a better lifestyle, or a Gogo for more money. So it makes sense that these places would fill themselves with girls directly out of Isan who don't know any better and don't speak good enough English to be able to handle themselves at a bar. Because of this you can find some gems here. Bar fines are usually rare here, but they're available; the Mamasan will come up with some type of price so you can take the girl, and since it's a little more of an old-school Thailand vibe, they may even negotiate a week-long price if you're interested. You'll also find some veterans on Soi 6, although I'm not really sure why. These girls will be willing to exchange phone numbers and meet you after work to avoid the bar fines. There are a couple of "lady boy"-only bars and there are a couple of bars that seem to be very pro-oral as far as their services go. At such places, some craziness might happen even before you make it upstairs; IF you make it upstairs.

Soi 6 is the ultimate daytime adventure, and when you leave you're practically on the beach with the rest of the day ahead of you, and all for 1,000 baht. Can't complain about that! You can also go to Soi 6 at night, but past midnight I don't think there's much going on there. Also, many of the nearby sois that connect the second road to the beach offer similar services, but none is as obvious or as crazy as Soi 6.

You'll also find just about any activity you're looking for in Pattaya. It's only 30 baht to take a boat to Koh Larn which is a beautiful island nearby. You can have an incredible hike up to the highest point on Koh Larn. You'll find everything you need in Pattaya, including movie theatres, shopping malls, bowling, Western food etc. Pattaya has a little bit of everything. Pattaya Beach isn't all that nice, but Jomtien has a nice beach and you can take a baht bus for 10 baht to get there!

There's another action-packed road called Soi Buakhao which has a little bit of everything. Prices on Soi Buakhao tend to be good and there's a lot of massage parlors and bars in the area.

Pattaya has so many women that they have to be somewhat competitive about their pricing. Pattaya is one of those places where you can get by for very little, but you can find ways to spend a lot if you're not being careful. I think it's actually pretty cheap for things like hotels, rent, food, girls, and bar prices. Go to a Western restaurant or to one of the nice discos or Gogos and things won't be so cheap. Also, the soapy massage parlors are the most affordable in Thailand; any motorbike taxi driver can take you to one if you ask. It's got a great blend of everything and I'll admit that it's my favorite place.

Bangkok

Bangkok is good in small doses. It's a dirty and congested city, but it has everything you could ever need in terms of entertainment, food, business, shopping, and culture. Nice hotels are expensive and it may take some walking around to find a decent deal, maybe 1,100 baht for a room that's half-way decent, but nothing special. Food is as cheap or expensive as your heart desires, depending on the decor and the cuisine of the restaurant. The ladies and bar fines are similar, if not slightly

higher than Pattaya. But, some girls in Bangkok are known to be good at getting more for their services than in Pattaya.

Nana, Soi Cowboy, and Patpong are your best bet for bars and Gogos. Any tuk tuk or taxi will be able to take you to any of those three places upon request. Ratchadipisek is another entertainment spot but I see mostly Asians there and it's not so "farang-friendly." If you're looking for a stunner and willing to pay 5,000 baht for two hours, Ratchadipisek might actually be your best bet though, in spite of it not being ideal for farang. You'd be hard-pressed to check out every place in those four entertainment centers if you had a year to do nothing but.

Bangkok is a lot to handle, and I recommend it for a couple days max. From there, someone on vacation should head either North to Chiang Mai, south to Phuket or other islands, or to nearby Pattaya. Living in Bangkok is difficult too, but the best jobs are there. Anyone who does live there would need to visit some islands frequently, just to get a break from all of the commotion. Also, women in Bangkok probably favor wealthy Asian men, so you might not be as sought-after as you would be in other places. Don't miss out on a legendary soapy massage if you can help it.

Phuket

If you're looking for beautiful beaches and women, you'll probably want to head for Phuket. It's a large island all the way south and it's filled with resorts, bars, and beaches. Really, if you're in Phuket I recommend going to a few different places. Patong Beach is a busy and decent beach during the day and this is the main hot spot at night. With all the girls, bars, and Gogos you can handle, Patong has an impressive nightlife. I find Patong's prices on food, alcohol, and beer to be more expensive than say Pattaya, but it's not terribly expensive as long as you're not going to the most expensive places. Even the bar fines aren't that bad. It's the girls themselves that tend to think they can get more in Patong and that has little to do with the way they look. There are a lot of elderly rich men who visit and pay big money, so some of the women tend to be a little spoiled and they don't seem to be so concerned with having competition. Don't let them treat you like you're on your death bed; they're lucky to have an opportunity to be with you! Use the rules in the book and just figure that Phuket is always a bit more expensive. I like when they ask for 300 baht for a ride home when I know they live in walking distance. Don't get abused and you'll be fine.

The best thing about Phuket is that it's close to the most exotic beaches you'll ever see in your life. Make sure to go to Koh Lanta and/or Phi Phi. They're unbelievably gorgeous. You'll want to bring a girl with you, and if you're on a budget, search for a good bungalow, because lodging can get up there in price. Water sports and hiking in Phuket, or in some of the nearby islands, is world class.

Chiang Mai

The second-biggest city in Thailand, Chiang Mai is in the north of the country and has a milder climate. Prices are very low on almost everything, and foreigners from the West are greatly appreciated by women. There's an active but not crazy night life, and you can see some beautiful waterfalls and jungle scenery. It won't be difficult to find where the main entertainment centers are where you'll find a slew of lady bars. They're on Moon Muang Road and at the Night Bazaar. It's nothing like Pattaya or Bangkok, and the bars are fairly quiet. I really like the girls in Chiang Mai as they seem to be a little less professional and a little more real. A lot of prostitutes in the region cater to Thai men, and there is an HIV problem because, supposedly, these men don't like to use condoms and are obliged. It's a big issue, so you want to be as safe as can be, and if you wind up spending more than just a night with a girl, get her tested. I find that a lot of the bar girls or even non-bar-girl local women are very eager to have a Western boyfriend.

You can have a great time drinking at a bar along the Ping River, which is a true Thai experience. Shopping is great in Chiang Mai thanks to amazing prices. But you should still negotiate! You'll find less Western food available per soi than in other regions, but they're out there if you look. Soapy Massage is available but it's kind of expensive, considering how cheap other things are in the area.

Koh Samuit

is more of a vacation spot for you and a Western woman, maybe even for a honeymoon. Some people disagree with me, but I know those on a budget won't. Koh Samuit is too damn expensive. Sure it's beautiful, but I've seen better in Thailand for cheaper. Don't get me wrong, it's got everything you need, including bars and plenty of available women. It's actually a little lower-key there and I noticed a lot of men with Thai girls for multiple days as "vacation companions." From talking to many of the girls, I know a lot of these guys get suckered into giving 30,000-baht tips at the end of their vacation, so these women are spoiled by ignorant vacationers. The guy's think they have earned respect or love with that money, but they don't get either. The woman just hopes she can get his email address and get him for a monthly stipend too. Between the high prices, the spoiled bar girls, and the lack of girls who aren't bar girls, it's just not my kind of island. You can use it as a jump-off point, though, to get to Koh Pangan, which I'll cover next.

Koh Phangan

is internationally known for its Full Moon Party, and nothing is really like it. The Full Moon Party is a mix of European men and women with some Thai's sprinkled in. It's really just a massive party and you'll find girls, a lot of booze, and offers of drugs. There are lots of setups and stings in relation to the drugs, with many people buying from an undercover, and that turns into a whole nightmare. Stick to the booze and you'll have a great time. It's once a month and you can take the boat from Koh Samuit for cheap to get there. The beach turns into a huge toilet bowl that night, which is annoying. There is also some partying the night or two before. It's something everyone should experience once.

Koh Chang

is located in the Eastern portion of the Gulf of Thailand about four hours from Pattaya (which includes a boat ride from Trat). Koh Chang is in the process of being developed into an island that can accommodate many more vacationers than it has in the past. For a couple of years in a row it seems like the amount of resorts and shopshas doubled annually. I love the island and I think it has a lot going for itself.

The water is gorgeous and unique. I can't say it's as beautiful as say Koh Lanta or Phi Phi; it's not. But its close enough to Bankok and Pattaya, and it's certainly the most beautiful place you'll find that is not in the Southern leg of Thailand. Across the gulf and heading south-west from Koh Chang by boat, you'd hit Koh Samuit which is north east of Phuket.

Koh Chang has cheap bungalows and some cheap hotels, but there are expensive resorts that have popped up as well that charge 8,000 baht per night. You can do well in the 1,000 to 1,500-baht-per-night range if you look, but you probably won't have any English channels on your TV, so load up your laptop with some movies. You can find some bungalows pretty much for half of that on the beach, but they won't have AC or TV.

It's a big island and there are many towns along the tourist side of the island. From the ferry station, you'll be on the northern tip and you'll soon get to "White Sand Beach", which is a little pricey but has great restaurants and a good night life with some live music and a section of lady bars called, "Little Pattaya." My recommendation is to take a lady with you to any island, but you can actually get away with coming to Koh Chang alone. Heading south you'll find a lot of great towns that get more and more beautiful, private, and expensive for transportation.

Koh Chang has great snorkeling, diving, hiking, and boating activities. Compared to other islands, the prices are cheap, but it's still an island, so the average meal will cost more than in Pattaya. Koh Chang is ideal for a long weekend if you're bringing a girl you're crazy about. I'd also go alone for two nights if I really wanted to relax; I'd be able to find company without a problem, but also without a terrific selection.

Koh Tao

is a gorgeous island without much action, and is the best bet for any divers or for people who want a romantic vacation.

Khao Yai

is a huge national park close enough to Bangkok. You can take a day-tour there to see amazing waterfalls and wildlife. It's a beautiful place and the location is fairly convenient. One full day should be enough to fill up your camera with things you won't see at home. Beware the elephants; they don't care about what's in their way when they're on a jog.

Krochanaburi

is a wonderful location in the western part of the country next to Burma. I recommend it as an

overnight trip, but no longer than two days and one night. Erewan Falls is one of the most breathtaking things I have seen in my life. It's just an amazing set of waterfalls with gorgeous blue water. You can book a front-to-back tour, but you might be better off taking a van shuttle there and just finding a hotel along the river, as they're cheap and there's good enough food nearby. Then you can do a day-tour where you'll see the Bridge over the River Kwai, a cave, and the War Cemetery.

Chapter 14: GAY/BI-SEXUAL/WOMEN/COUPLES

The tourist destinations of Pattaya, Bangkok, and Phuket are filled with just about any combination of sexual offering one can think of. Gay and bi-sexual men can feel totally uninhibited in these spots and will have numerous bars and Gogo's that specifically entertain them. Men looking to be with lady boys will find no shortage to pick from. There isn't even a large difference in the way you would go about picking them up at bars and discos compared to the women. Their rates tend to be slightly cheaper but this also depends on the "quality" of the lady boy. Lady boy street-walkers are not recommended as they have been known to cause most of the petty-theft crimes in the pay-for-play industry. With the strength of a man it can be difficult to fight one off, so you need to use caution. There are plenty of establishments you can find where lady boys are more accountable to their bar/Gogo, and the bar fine is well worth the peace of mind. There are also plenty of gay establishments with gay men, and not lady boys, working at a bar or a disco. It won't take much Google action to find out where to go, and they are often in clusters. Pattaya may be more impressive overall to a gay man than to a straight man, because there's just no comparing the amount of gay-friendly, affordable pay-for-play venues in Pattaya to any other place in the world. The straight bars/club's still out-number the gay ones maybe by three to one, but a gay man will certainly have his hands full with much less competition vying for the attention of Thai men they are attracted to. It should be known that many of the "gay pay-for-play specialists" might not be as gay as they come off, and many of them are supporting a family.

There are many instances where a bi-sexual or gay man isn't able to be himself in his home country, and he may even be married. Many men in those situations come out to Thailand knowing that all of their escapades will be affordable and discreet, thousands of miles away from anyone who they know. Many of the same rules apply, so if you're gay and you skipped right to this chapter, you're going to want to read most of the other chapters to know how to handle yourself against traps and scams. Certainly there are a lot of men who "sponsor" a Thai man in just the same way as it is for the ladies, and my opinion remains the same: do not give anyone money unless you are actually with them in person.

Same-sex marriage is still not recognized by the Thai government, but they have passed some laws within the last decade that speak well to a gay-friendly view, such as removing a ban on admittance into the military. A gay couple might also hit a lot of road blocks adopting a baby in Thailand, and it's not easy even for straight foreigners to accomplish that. Phuket, Pattaya, and Bangkok are the most gay-friendly cities, and a gay man would find no major issues settling down in those cities either as a single man who dates, or settling down in a long-term relationship. HIV and AIDS are prevalent in the Thai gay community, so testing and condoms are an absolute must. Gay men can't even be blood donors in Thailand because of this issue.

Certain straight couples who want to explore a third partner for sex, or even for companionship, will also find this relatively easy, and can avoid the negative repercussions that might come of this in their home country. I have talked to numerous Thai girls who have had experiences with couples, and it's not uncommon for a retired couple to live here with a Thai girl. I have seen it all here, including straight couples who bar-fine a lady boy for a week. What might be considered devious in the West, may be par for the course here. And what I like about that is that it's really only when it comes to sex. In terms of crime or drugs or truly anti-establishment behavior, Thailand is like any other Western country. It's just very loose about sex and sexual orientation and even trans-gender. Speaking of which, people do travel to Thailand for gender-reassignment surgery because of the vast experience some of the surgeons have here in it, and because of the low prices. If this is something you or someone you know is interested in, be sure to find as reputable a doctor as you can.

Lesbians from the West aren't totally unheard of here either, and can find happiness in much the same way that a gay man or a straight man can. There aren't any lesbian Gogo's, but it wouldn't take long or much asking around for a woman to find an interested playmate. Actually this is considerably more common than women coming here looking for Thai men, which is very rare. I don't see it as being a bad option for an older straight lady who is unhappy and lonely. They can come here, perhaps with a small pension or retirement social-security payment or fund, and have no problem meeting someone and living a nice life. Supposedly there has been a very recent uptick in single and perhaps fairly young women coming to Thailand and paying for gigolo services. They can go to the same gay establishments to find men that will happily go both ways for cash.

Chapter 15: DRUGS, ALCOHOL, AND STD

Narcotics

Thailand used to be a large player in the Emerald Triangle's drug production business, thanks in part to the climate adequately suiting the growth of the poppy plant which is used in making opiates such as heroin. Fortunately it isn't nearly as prevalent as it used to be, and much of that business still exists in nearby countries such as Burma. Like anywhere else, of course, there is still some hardcore narcotic production and distribution in Thailand, but the harsh laws against possession, and the incredibly harsh laws against distribution, keep most farang out of the cycle. So most hardcore narcotics in Thailand these days are usually some type of methamphetamine that is smoked, such as "ice" or "yaba", better known in the West as "speed" or "crystal." They're extremely addictive and cheap to make, and they're prevalent in the Gogo industry.

If you have a drug problem you are going to want to stay away from Thailand. Bumping into the wrong freelancer with access to "ice" is going to put you on a bad path with consequences far worse than where the temptations of drug use might quickly lead you in your home country. If you're caught with hard drugs you could wind up spending a nice chunk of your life in a jail that would make the worst American jails seem like a vacation. I'm not going to preach to you about getting help; that's not my job. If you do drugs, that is your right; just don't do them in Thailand. And if you don't trust yourself totally to avoid them here, then you need to avoid Thailand.

Marijuana

"Ganja," as it's often referred to here, is naturally not on the same page as Ice when it comes to its dangers to the body or to the legal system in Thailand. However, technically there are still harsh laws when it comes to marijuana, many times tougher than in any Western country. How often those laws are enforced is up to debate. Certainly the distribution of marijuana in Thailand is very harshly penalized to the tune of something bad enough to realistically mess up your life forever. Possession of a small amount of marijuana in Thailand will usually result in paying some sort of "fine", but the laws here seem to allow the punishment to be devised by whoever you might face if you're caught with it. So there may be a good chance that you just pay a fine if you're caught with a little ganja, but it's not certain. And even a weekend in a Thai jail will be the worst thing that ever happens to you. Bringing any drugs across borders in Asia is the easiest way to ruin your life. And the bottom line on all drugs, including marijuana, is that it's not good to involve yourself with them when you're anywhere in Asia. I will say that I have been surprised by the amount of farang who live here who smoke the stuff; it's a big number.

Steroids/HGH

I would never give advice on things that you should only consult with a doctor or lawyer about. But I will tell you what I know so that it might better prepare you for how to go about getting the proper information for yourself.

It doesn't seem as though Thailand is harsh on the personal consumption of anabolic steroids and similar chemicals. If it was I suspect they would be less available then they currently are, because currently you can get them in many over-the-counter pharmacies. All popular anabolic steroids are common in Thailand. Many are fake and it's going to be hard for you to tell, so buyer beware. It's also completely out of the question to get involved in the distribution as it is punished in the same way that distribution of other drugs is. There is no question that there are many steroid users here, especially in Bangkok and Pattaya, and that the "geared-up individuals" have an easy time getting it for cheap. There is even some talk amongst body builders that Pattaya, specifically, can be a body-building haven for a few months at a time. But when you are putting chemicals into your body that cause extreme reactions, it doesn't sound like a good idea to experiment with something that you don't know is totally legitimate, and that would be my fear if I was inclined to try it here. I believe the law states that you need a prescription to have them, so there is no point in taking any risks, the biggest of which would be crossing borders with it. Do not under any circumstance try to cross borders with steroids, even if you have a prescription. HGH is very hard to get here but some people swear by the stuff.

Supplement shops are common in Thailand. If you go to body-building shops in Bangkok or in Pattaya, you can probably find some extremely capable supplements that you know are legitimate and that you know are legal here. You may not gain 20 kilos of muscle in a month, but you'll make gains and you won't put your heart through the wringer. So if you want to take shortcuts hassle-free and safely, use some strong supplements and avoid anabolic steroids.

Cialis/Viagra/Painkillers

Technically you need a doctor's note to get any of these three, but Cialis and Viagra are probably taken as often as Tylenol here, so it's not hard to find it at all. Many places have signs in the windows and will sell them to you no-questions-asked. The charge is about 500 baht per blue pill; Cialis seems to go for a bit more. And, surprise-surprise, there are copies and fakes out there too. Large pharmacies are more likely to sell you the real thing, but you should make sure they have the official packaging, and it would be nice if you could see them from when they are in the box. Some places will tell you they can sell you copies for cheap. This, like steroids, is a drug that causes an extreme reaction in your body, and you don't want to mess around with cheap stuff. If you're much older or you have a heart condition, naturally you should consult a doctor to see how your heart is doing before you go and make yourself feel swell. But the bottom line is, if you're coming here on vacation you probably don't need to bring any with you; you can worry about that when you get here and you won't really wind up worrying about anything. The number of farang in Thailand who use "The Pill" is off the charts. The pharmacies go through boxes and boxes of the stuff.

Rehabilitation

Thailand does have numerous drug and alcohol rehabilitation centers, and some of these resemble the ones that Hollywood stars use. These luxury facilities might be a bargain in Thailand, so if you are in crisis you might want to Google around and see what is out there for you. If you do decide to rehab here, do not come here until you have already made prior arrangements guaranteeing you proper care from minute-one off of the plane. You do not want to come here and worry about finding one when you get here. There is a ridiculous amount of temptation here, unlike almost any place else, and without someone guiding you from the airport you might run into severe problems.

There is also an extreme rehabilitation method here that is somewhat internationally known. The Thamkrabok Monastery is basically a free rehab center administered by monks. You just have to pay minimally for food and everything else is provided for you. This is not a luxury rehab center and you will not be coddled here. From what I understand it is one of the most intense rehab centers out there and you cannot leave at any time while your rehab process is under way. They also make you take a vow to never take anything addictive ever again for the rest of your life. Perhaps this is the kind of thing some people need. More information can be found at http://www.thamkrabok.net/

STDs in Thailand

By the early 90s, HIV and AIDS were well on the rise in Thailand, and the government made an inspired commitment to stopping the trend by forcing people to get educated about the risks. Their "100% condom" campaign was seen as being highly successful, and is primarily responsible for Thailand not having an Africa-like epidemic. Of course I think safe sex is the way to go, and I suggest always using protection; it would be silly to suggest otherwise. I'm guessing my readers already have a good understanding of this concept and don't need me to elaborate.

The common misperception is that women in the farang pay-for-play industry have a great chance of getting HIV/AIDS. That is totally ridiculous and I'll explain why. It's estimated that a little less than 1per cent of people in the country have HIV or Aids. This is still three to five times higher than in most first world countries, so it's clearly still a problem here. I don't believe it is an epidemic though, because there is a disproportionate percentage of drug users and gay men/lady boys who have it. The facts point towards anal sex being significantly more risky than straight vaginal sex, possibly ten to twenty times as risky. And the sharing of needles is extremely risky. The percentage of gay men or lady boys in Thailand is considerably higher than in the Western countries, so if someone says that AIDS is a total epidemic in Thailand, that is true only in the gay population. It's still a problem outside of drug users and gay men, but not much more so than anywhere else. There are no exact numbers or facts when analyzing only males and females who never use needles and never have anal sex, but it's most likely less than half of one per cent. The biggest hot spot for AIDS among women, presumably in the pay-for-play industry, is up north in Chiang Mai. There the girls hardly ever use condoms and their customers are mostly Thai men, and you guessed it, Chiang Mai also has a reputation for having many drug users. So we know that drug users, people who have anal sex, and people in the Chiang Mai region have a much higher chance of having HIV/AIDS than other demographics. Some naïve people may say, "Fine, but the remaining people who have it are probably the farang prostitutes." This also isn't true. AIDS/HIV is prevalent deep into the country where there are no farang, and this is due in part to the rampant infidelity of Thai men. So if a Thai man uses a prostitute in the country, there's a decent chance no condom is used, and there's a decent chance he goes home to his wife or girlfriend after. Lady boys exist outside of the tourist spots as well, so somebody has to be using their services, right? Meanwhile, a large percentage of the farang bar-scene girls is using protection every time they have sex. So I think a logical conclusion to draw is that the farang bar girls in the tourist hot spot have about the same chance of having HIV as the national average, which would be around 1 per cent.

HIV/AIDS isn't something you contract easily from straight vaginal sex. So I think even more of a concern than HIV/AIDS are other STDs such as gonorrhea and Chlamydia. Unlike HIV, these two are very common in the bar-girl scene, and it's very easily contracted. If you have unprotected sex with a few women at the bars, I think you have a great chance of getting a problem. If you're unlucky or stupid enough to get caught in that situation (I have), then you'll most likely need to go to any of the pharmacies in Thailand and buy one of the most popular dugs in the world, zithromax/azythromycin. This will probably wipe out any case of Chlamydia or gonorrhea, but not before wrecking your body with short-term side effects. It sucks when your penis burns, so be smart. Clinics offer cheap testing, so if you have a girlfriend be sure to get her and yourself tested for everything. Then you won't be taking such a risk if a condom breaks or you forget to use one. In that case you only need to worry about pregnancy. With oral, the odds of getting anything go down by ten times, and to the best of my knowledge you can't get a girl pregnant from oral. Anal without a condom is about as risky as jumping off of a building.

One other note on this subject: there seems to be a consensus among ex-pats that bar girls are more willing to not use a condom than was the case even just a few years ago. This is a disturbing trend, although there is no proof that it exists. The best advice I can give you is this: in my experience some girls will absolutely always use a condom unless they have a long-term boyfriend, and that's fine. If a girl lets you go about your business without a condom, you're not the only lucky customer she did this for… and so you're really not very lucky at all, are you?

Chapter 16: FREQUENTLY ASKED QUESTIONS

Is Thailand dangerous? If you're not acting like an idiot and you stick to non-shady places, I find Thailand to be as safe as, or safer than, most urban cities in the West. The chances of having a problem while minding your own business are lower than in most places; however, if you're acting like a complete mess then I suppose the consequences in Thailand would be higher than in many places, especially if we consider that a stint in their jails is like a near-death sentence. Getting yourself out of a jam is fairly easy, thanks to the power of the dollar or euro. If you're always respectful, the chances of you being in a dangerous situation are as low as can be. If anyone bothers you while you're minding your own business, it would likely be another farang.

The biggest dangers are the motorbikes and driving drunk, but that shouldn't come as a surprise to anyone. Jungle treks tend to be safe; elephant trampling and deaths due to snakes are rare, although I can't say it absolutely never happens. You can get killed by a bear, scorpion or snake in some U.S. forests and deserts just the same.

Do I need a visa to enter Thailand? No, but if you intend to stay here for more than thirty days you might need to hop out and back in to extend to another fifteen days. If you intend to stay longer than that, you need to square away a long-term visa, which is explained in Chapter 9.

Do I tip in Thailand? This is an endless and agonizing debate with no perfect answer. Traditionally, Thailand is a non-tipping country, but it is expected that a farang leave a tip in many situations. A decent rule of thumb is 10 per cent, and you don't want it to get out of hand and start tipping at 20 and 25 per cent, like you may do at home sometimes. Although, if you had a meal served to you somewhere and it only came out to 80 baht, you can leave 100 total I suppose. The funny thing is that there is no wrong answer, but there often isn't a right answer either. Ten per cent, that'll do the trick. I tip higher at discos because it can take a while to get a drink if you're not a good tipper, and they'll give you a fuller shot if they know you take care of them.

Is HIV a big problem in Thailand? Chapter 19 breaks this down efficiently. The short answer is yes among gays or people that have anal sex or use drugs. It's a problem among straight people too, but not at epidemic levels or anything so much worse than in some first world countries.

Is English spoken commonly in Thailand? Enough English is spoken for you to get by in any of the touristy spots, and most of the women you're likely to meet in these same cities know at least some English. Thais are all taught English in school, but many of them don't adequately pick it up there. Hotels, restaurants, bars, discos, and any foreign-friendly establishments have an English speaker, just maybe not someone who is fluent.

Is all of the food too spicy? They can make anything much spicier than anyone should ever eat, but they can also easily make it non-spicy. They usually know to keep it mild for farang, so if you want spicy you'll need to request it, just the same as you would need to request non-spicy. It's not a real problem at all; the food is awesome and cheap in Thailand and everyone unanimously agrees.

Does the food get you sick? When you travel to different continents you can get sick easily, purely because your body is not used to handling completely different food. Are you more likely to get sick from the food in Thailand than, say, Australia? Yes. But not much more so than if you went to most places. If you're on vacation you should come equipped with stomach medications and anti-acids. You should also stay away from cheese in Thailand, which has been known to set people off. Thais don't use cheese much, so who knows how long they've had it in their refrigerator.

Is the water safe to drink? In the major cities it seems to be. But it's also cheap enough in bottles that you should only drink bottled water or from the filtered water machines.

Should I bring travelers' checks or cash or an ATM card? Travelers' checks are old school. ATM cards work all over Thailand so you should bring one as a backup. The charges are annoying though, so the easiest thing to do is to bring over as much of your own currency as you'll think you'll need. When you exchange big bills from your country you get a decent exchange rate from the currency exchanges that are located at or directly in front of banks.

When is the best time of the year to come? If you want to go island-hopping, the busy season, December through early April, is when the waters are the most calm. By mid-April you run into a heat wave and Songkran, a holiday that usually shuts down a large portion of the pay-for-play industry for a

few days. After the busy season there are fewer farang and prices go down on nearly everything, but some of the best-looking bar girls go back to their home towns. It rains in the late summer to early fall, and it rains a lot. If you're really into the beach scene you'll want to come during the busy season to avoid the worst of the heat, high tides, and rain. If you are coming just for the girls or you want to see the inner country, come off-peak.

Are there a lot of political problems there like we saw on TV in Bangkok in the Spring of 2010?
The news channels tend to sensationalize things and bloviate. No ex-pats and travelers were really in DANGER when that was going on for a couple of days. And since then it's been fine. There are perhaps some long-term issues, but the Thai military is not at any risk from any type of rebellious action. In 2010, it was sling-shot vs. machine gun and you can guess who won that. This tells me that there is no problem the Thai military can't quickly dispatch, and I think problems are unlikely anyhow. Certainly in any event there is no animosity towards foreigners, so this shouldn't be a factor in any decision you make concerning Thailand.

Is there Western-style hospital care in Thailand?
In the big cities, absolutely and it's cheap. But as you can imagine, the small villages don't have proper facilities due to a lack of funds. Dentists in the major cities are also very good and cheap. And many people come to Thailand for the low price on plastic surgery.

Is Thailand a good place to go to alone? It's an amazing destination for the solo traveler. You'll meet a companion on day-one if you want to, and you'll be able to make friends with other travelers fairly easily, and especially if you go on a tour.

If I need help, what do I do? The tourist police are there for you; they speak English and can be quite helpful in every city. You can also easily get in touch with your embassy.

What is the weather like, aside from the obvious? It can be brutally hot in the late spring and early summer season, but I don't think anyone has ever had a bad time due to the heat. The heat is more a factor at night because you might sweat when you're walking around. Those that live here get used to the heat after some time. The rain is a pain in the ass sometimes, but typically Thailand has great vacation weather and would be hard to beat for retirement. It's a bit cooler up north, which can be nice sometimes.

Can I backpack through Thailand? It's a popular destination for backpackers, thanks to the cheap rents of bungalows and the variety of inexpensive activities.

What do I need to know about The King? That he is perhaps as beloved by the Thai people more than any other figure is by a country in the modern world. They obviously love this man for a reason, and loving Thailand as much as I do, I guess I can be thankful for what he has done as well. The last thing you want to do in Thailand is say anything negative about the King, or disrespect anything symbolic of him or that has his picture on it.

What impact does Buddhism have on people? No religion is perfect but Buddhism is close. It seems to help people focus on things we can all agree are positive, such as peace and tranquility. If there is a negative, it is that too many people take reincarnation seriously to the point of justifying things like unsafe sex and bad-driving habits. Some girls literally think to themselves that if they get AIDS and die that they'll just come back again and maybe have a better opportunity for happiness.

They don't take things too seriously, which is good, but sometimes they need to take things more seriously than they do. Again, no religion or philosophy is perfect, and I am just pointing out the couple of issues Westerners might find confusing. There seems to be a bit of justification for infidelity based on a Buddhist principle that says something that could loosely be translated as, "whatever you don't know doesn't hurt." If someone uses Buddhism to create excuses for doing things that are foolish, then they really aren't practicing it properly, but you get your fair share of that here. I can point to some other religions that have caused 100-year wars, massacres etc. Buddhism is mostly peace and tranquility, with just a little unfortunate justification problem that comes as a result of poor interpretation by people looking for excuses. Meditation is not necessarily a religious experience, although it is a part of Buddhism. Studies show that it can extend your life, so it is a wonderful thing people can do here at some temples in breathtakingly beautiful places.

What's with all of the homeless dogs?

I think most countries have abandoned dogs; I think most countries put these dogs in the pound where most are euthanized. In Thailand they don't get euthanized; I suppose the Buddhist mentality is to let them be. I'm a dog lover so I find this to be compassionate, but I realize there is also a downside which is many hungry dogs on the streets. I find it interesting to see them in action sometimes. Their survival skills are impressive, as many of them have learned to cross busy streets the same way people do, and many of them have claimed a certain area or territory for themselves where they can count on getting food and water from some nice people who live nearby, or by people who are passing through and feeling generous. As it pertains to the traveler, you don't have to be scared of the homeless dogs in the busy cities and tourist hot-pots. Part of the dogs' survival depends on them not having issues with any people, and they seem to have figured this out. There may be exceptions to any rule, but I have never seen or heard about a dog attacking someone in the streets that wasn't provoking a problem. I suppose the most dangerous thing about the dogs might be if they are being careless in the streets and cause a motorbike accident. If you want to feed a dog just buy him a stick of pork from a street vendor and throw it to them, they know how to eat it without eating the stick. You're better off not petting the dogs because they're dirty, and in rare cases they can have rabies or something else nasty.

Can I bring my a girlfriend/wife from the West to Thailand with me?
Sure, you guys can have honeymoon-like vacations here for relatively cheap, so I recommend it. If she's into women, you can have a hell of a vacation, but I think you could have a great time even if she's not. On more than a few occasions you might wish you were alone, but you'll manage.

Is Thailand good for children?
If I had children I would take them to Thailand on a vacation, but I wouldn't want them to be anywhere near the streets with bar girls. But there are a lot of activities for children in the major beach cities and they'll get a kick out of any sight-seeing tours, snorkeling tours, or mild jungle tours. I would only go when the waters are calm (think busy season).

Is it easy to adopt a baby from Thailand?   No, it might be trendy, but it certainly isn't easy, and nearby countries might make more sense for doing this. The process can take over a year, which eliminates the opportunity to adopt a newborn, and it can be a frustrating endeavor which could include multiple trips before you are successful.

Is Thailand filled with pedophiles?   Let me be clear about one thing: nothing in my mind can be more heinous than a man sexually abusing young children. This has been a well-known problem in South-East Asia for many decades, but fortunately it is getting better by leaps and bounds, especially in Thailand. They are now prosecuting harshly in some cases, and the general acceptance level amongst the people is down considerably. The age of consent is tricky, with some stating it to be 15 or 16, but with sex with anyone under 18 also being punishable by law. STICK TO 18+ with no exceptions. With drugs, I told people if they can't stop doing them just don't come to Thailand where the consequences are far worse. If you like young boys and girls, I hope you get into a car accident on the way to the airport; a very bad car accident.

Is making porn illegal?   Some people mistake the lenient attitude on prostitution in Thailand for being across-the-board when it comes to all things sex. Making any kind of porn is illegal, and many have been fined and deported for doing so.

What do I do if I eat something way too spicy or I get food poisoning?   If you eat something so spicy that you can't handle yourself, you should drink something hot, like hot tea immediately. I'm not a scientist so I can't explain why it works, but it does, and cold water does nothing. With food poisoning, you need to eat plain toast and real yogurt and drink only water. Stomach pills often just irritate the situation, and Tylenol will make things worse as well. Real yogurt (not the sugar-filled flavored type) works wonders for food poisoning and can save you if you're traveling.

I'm a rookie, where should I go?   If you love the beach, head down to Phuket. If you just want to be with a lot of women, Pattaya is your place. If you like rivers and waterfalls and cheap prices you'll enjoy Chiang Mai.

Chapter 17: RESOURCES THAT WILL HELP YOU

*** I only endorse two businesses in Thailand and I won't even list them in the book since this isn't ad space.

1)   If you need a very affordable and old-school match-maker in Isan to find you a beautiful non-bar girl as a long-term spouse or wife, please let me know and I'll get you the details.

2)   If you're under 50 and you think you're going to run into visa issues, I know a place that has the perfect solution.

So if you want to talk further about either of these two things, make sure you email me at: info@thaigirlspattayagirls.com

The following are not advertisements; you have my word that I don't have arrangements with any of the links below. These are just the best resources that I have put together over the course of doing more research and internet surfing than anyone should ever have to do on their own.

Translating and communicating in Thai:
http://translate.google.com/#   (easily translates English into Thai)
http://www.gate2home.com/?language=th (type Thai, then copy and paste into Google translator.

Messageboards:
http://www.thaivisa.com/forum/
http://www.pattayasecrets.com/forums/
http://www.pattaya-addicts.com/forum/
http://www.phuket-info.com/forums/
http://www.ajarn.com/ (has forum for teachers)

Guides for Gogo's/massage/lady bars:
http://www.pattayagogos.com/index.htm
http://www.pattayaagogos.net/
http://www.pattayagogoreview.com/
http://www.davetheravebangkok.com/category/go-go-bars/
http://www.phuket.com/nightlife/go-go-bars.htm
http://www.phuket-info.com/forums/

General information and free sites with stories and opinions:

/www.stickmanbangkok.com/living.html
p://www.1stopbangkok.com
ttp://www.pattayanewbie.com/
http://www.bangkokguidebook.com/

Private investigator for background checks:
http://www.pattaya-investigations.com/
http://www.thailandpi.com/
http://www.thailandpi.com/thai-girlfriend-investigations.htm (case studies from investigations).

Highly regarded activities/tours:
http://www.phuket.com/tours/10mustdo.htm (Phuket)
http://www.kosamui.com/tours/tours-top10.htm (Koh Samuit)
http://www.chiangmai-grouptours.com/day_tour.php (Chiang Mai)
http://www.pattaya.bangkok.com/tours/top-ten.htm (Pattaya)
http://www.bangkok.com/tours-top10.htm (Bangkok)
http://www.i-sitekohchang.com/koh-chang-tours/tours.html (Koh Chang)
http://www.cavelodge.com/mbike.htm (Mountain Biking)

Interactive maps of each city:
http://www.sawadee.com/map/

Tourist Police:
Dial 1155

List of the embassies found in Bangkok by country with address and phone
http://www.th4u.com/embassies.htm#usa

Most-trusted lawfirms:
http://www.sunbeltlegaladvisors.com/
http://www.siam-legal.com/

Best hotel website:
http://www.hotels2thailand.com/

Restaurant guide:
http://www.dininginthailand.com/
Movie theatre guide:
http://www.movieseer.com/th/index.aspx

2012 Holiday schedule (not much variation year to year)
Christmas and New Years Eve and Day are celebrated in the tourist spots.

Makha Bucha
Makha Bucha celebrates the Buddha's first sermon.
Wednesday, 7 March 2012

info@thaigirlspattayagirls.com

Chakri Day
Chakri Day celebrates the founding of the present dynasty by King Rama I.
Friday, 6 April 2012

Songkran
Songkran is the traditional Thai New Year when Thailand becomes one big water festival. Conveniently scheduled during a very hot time of the year, it's unlike anything you've ever seen before. It lasts for almost a week, but each city has one day in which everything closes down for the water festival, and it can be a different day for each city, so you'll want to ask around to know when your destination city is having their "Big Day."

Friday, 13 April 2012
Saturday, 14 April 2012
Sunday, 15 April 2012
Monday, 16 April 2012 (Substitute)
Tuesday, 17 April 2012 (Substitute)

Coronation Day
Commemorates the day when King Rama IX was crowned in 1949.
Saturday, 5 May 2012

Visakha Bucha / Vesak Day
The day the Buddha was born and the holiest Buddhist holiday.
Monday, 4 June 2012

Buddhist Lent Day (Wan Khao Phansa)
Friday, 3 August 2012

H.M. The Queen's Birthday
and **Mother's Day**
Sunday, 12 August 2012
Monday, 13 August 2012(Substitute)

Chulalongkorn Memorial Day
A day to remember King Rama V.
Tuesday, 23 October 2012

Loy Krathong 2012
Wednesday, 28 November 2012

H.M. The King's Birthday

Wednesday, 5 December 2012

Thai Constitution Day
Inaugural day of the Thai constitution.
Monday, 10 December 2012

Chapter 18: CONCLUSION

If you have come this far, I feel good about your chances of not falling into the typical traps that so many men do in Thailand. I know that some people will say I have been a little negative. I think I've just been totally realistic, and there's a lot to look out for with women all over the world, so it isn't like Thailand has more negatives than any other place. I love Thailand, I live here. Yes, I have warned you about many things, and perhaps even scared you about a couple of things, but what can be more of a positive endorsement for a place than saying the following:

If you come to Thailand and you know what you're doing you will be able to live like a king.

You've read the book; you know what you're doing. Whether you come to stay here long-term or you just come for a vacation, you're set to have an amazing and a life-changing experience here. It's not going to go that way for every guy that comes here. The ones that don't understand the ins and outs may end up giving all their money to a bar lady or getting arrested for doing drugs. Meanwhile you'll be enjoying some of the most beautiful places, best food, and exotic women the world has to offer, without a care in the world.

People can say that any place can be terrible or great, and that it's all about what you make of it. There's truth there, but it's especially poignant in Thailand. From the cautious guy who lives like a millionaire on 60,000 baht a month, to the guy who lost it all to a bar girl or on a silly business deal, there is a huge discrepancy between people who go about things the right and wrong way. I just think there are quality-of-life opportunities that exist only in this country. There are other countries with cheap women, to be sure, but, Thailand gives you a little of everything else, including, Western amenities, gorgeous beaches, and a lot of ex-pats you can be friends with.

Someone once told me that living in Thailand can be like living in a casino: you can get a lot of complimentary meals and you can have a great time, but if you stay too long the house will always win and you'll always lose. After he said that, I asked the man if he had a long-term relationship with a bar girl, and sure enough he said he was married to one and it was a huge disaster. He made mistakes and he screwed up, but it doesn't have to be that way. He could have met a wonderful woman, but for some strange reason he convinced himself that a prostitute would make for a suitable wife. He would never have made the same mistake in his own country, but he fell into the same trap in Thailand that so many do. I just can't say enough about it because it happens to so many thousands of men every month. For every five fools who fall into the bar-girl trap, there is one man who is careful and follows the rules… one very happy man. There will be some men who come here after reading this book and say again and again, "Wow, good thing I know better." Unfortunately there will be some men who read this book and say, "It's different with this girl; she's the exception and I just want to help her and her family." There's clearly nothing more that I can do or say to help someone like that, but I will say that he'd have been better off not coming to Thailand at all.

I'm clearly not a professional writer and I apologize if some of the grammatical errors in the book were a nuisance to you. If I was a professional writer I probably wouldn't be in a position to have been able to learn as much as I have about this place, and the quality of the information in it wouldn't have been as good.

A FEW LAST TIPS

You want to know a stupid ice-breaker that seems to work when you're at bar? Tell them that they can bar-fine you for free tonight. It's the dumbest thing in the world but it makes them laugh and it makes the "bar fine" topic a little easier to discuss.

You want to know a stupid ice-breaker that seems to work when a pretty girl is walking by you? Tell her, "Where you go?" This is what many ladies say to Thai men as they pass, and you're bound to hear it 100 times a week in Thailand. When you say this to a bar lady that is walking by you, she'll certainly laugh out loud and you can get her phone number if you like.

Learn how to tell women that they're beautiful in Thai ("Kun suay mak"). The worse your Thai pronunciation is the more they'll appreciate the compliment.

If you visit a Buddhist temple, that is your best bet for making a charitable donation. The monks are used to getting 20, 50, or 100 baht from people who visit. Give 1,000 baht as they can be trusted to do good things with the money compared to other charities. A lot of the monks speak English and they're very interesting people. I don't find it to be a religious experience; it's more spiritual than anything else. I'm no hippie, believe me; but there's something about those old Buddhist temples and meditating at one. Give it a shot.

Don't discriminate against a friend if he bar-fines the occasional lady boy. When I saw one of my friends do this for the first time I was so shocked and I tried to save him. I shouted, "That's not a Woman!" He said, "Mike, I know. It's OK. Sometimes I go with a lady boy. I'm not gay. It's fine." Baffled, I just kept saying, "Really?" I was a rookie to the scene and I wasn't used to such things back in the U.S. I avoided his phone call and I wasn't sure if I wanted to hang out with the guy after that. But that was ridiculous really. It's not like the man did anything wrong or inappropriate. Who cares what he does in his own bedroom. I called him after a few weeks and apologized for my behavior. Truthfully, he's got to be at least a little gay and it's perfectly fine that he doesn't see it that way. Gay or not, it doesn't matter to me because he's a great guy. If I refused to hang out with anyone who's ever been with a lady boy my options would run pretty dry and I'd have missed out on having good times with some excellent people. I'm not into it, I don't understand it, and it confuses me. But I have come to a healthy place where I don't judge either the lady boy or anyone who sees a lady boy for doing what they do. With the amount of women I've been with here, who am I to judge?

You may be tempted to check out China, Japan, and Taiwan while you're in Asia. Don't expect to meet women in those countries. It could happen, but I'd avoid the prostitutes all together, and the regular gals are either shy or hard to get. Vietnam, Cambodia, Laos, and the Philippines are the opposite and they're cheap, and the places are easy to get to from Thailand. I don't find those countries to be as well-rounded as Thailand, not even close. But if you're a traveler and you really like Asian women, those countries are certainly worth a look.

Certain websites are blocked in Thailand. There are programs out there such as "Ghost Surf" that let you get around this inconvenience. You won't miss the news and propaganda sites that are blocked, and there's no reason you'd need porn. It's more or less just something for professional gamblers to deal with since many of the sports books and poker sites are blocked. China blocks Facebook and a lot of other sites, so Thailand isn't even close to the worst when it comes to censorship.

Well that should do it. Make the most of your experience here, but don't exploit people or get exploited by people. I hope you enjoyed the book. I know it's more of a guide than it is an enjoyable read, but hopefully there were moments for you where you lost track of time as you got into it. My goal was just to make sure that you know how to make the most of your opportunities here, and how to avoid the issues so many ignorant guys face. I hope I've accomplished my goal. No matter how much you know about the system, if you can't handle temptation I guess it wouldn't matter much anyway. Be smart, be careful, and be safe.

Thanks for reading.

22232942R10078

Made in the USA
Lexington, KY
19 April 2013